RESILIENCE DO-OVER

VICTORIA V. MOYA

RESILIENCE DO-OVER

*How to Rediscover Yourself
and Access Innate Strength
to Face Hardships*

VICTORIA V. MOYA

PASSIONPRENEUR®
PUBLISHING

Publishing information
Publishing and design facilitated by
Passionpreneur Publishing
A division of Passionpreneur Organization Pty Ltd
ABN: 48640637529

Melbourne, VIC | Australia
www.passionpreneurpublishing.com

To my father, the Boss
Your love transcends time and holds
me up in hardships.
You are still my rockstar, my hero
for all my life, Enkosi Siyoyo.
And
To my mom
Mampondo, your compassion was the glue that
kept me from breaking, and your love knew no
bounds, Enkosi Manyawuza.

TESTIMONIALS

Powerful novels of heroes overcoming adversity are still read a thousand years later. This is because they have a positive effect on our self-belief and can drive us to achieve better lives than we believed possible.

Victoria's book will do the same for its readers and more. This is a beautifully told and thoughtful account of her rise to business success. From the start of this brutally honest book to the insights into management, Victoria's strong, confident voice comes through. Having worked with her as a consultant, I can attest to the successes she attributes to the personal growth she achieved through adversity, thoughtfulness and perseverance.

All who read this book will be pleased they did."

—Ian Mann
Bestselling Author of 'Managing with Intent'
&Founder of Gateways Business Consultants

"I am thrilled to write this testimonial for Victoria Moya, a respected franchisee of McDonald's South Africa and now a published author.

Her book is a testament to her resilience, determination, and unwavering grit. Throughout her journey, she has displayed unparalleled bravery and persistence, overcoming challenges with a level-headed leadership style that inspires all who work alongside her.

Yet, amidst the trials, her caring nature and zestful, spirited heart shine through, bringing joy and positivity to all she encounters. Her story is a beacon of hope and a reminder that with perseverance and a dash of fun, anything is possible."

—Greg Solomon
CEO McDonald's SOUTH AFRICA.

As a business leader and life coach, Victoria has truly been a guiding light, helping me navigate through challenges and unlocking my full potential. Her expertise and insights have been invaluable in shaping my career and personal growth. Her guidance has helped me set clear goals, develop effective strategies, and overcome obstacles along the way.

Beyond her professional expertise, Victoria's genuine care and compassion have made our coaching sessions feel like a safe space for growth and self-reflection. Her positive energy and enthusiasm are contagious, and enabling me to feel inspired and empowered.

—Thembisa Tyam
Divisional Head: SBV Services
(Mentee)

Victoria is a remarkably strong and resilient woman with a bois-terous personality. Her commanding spirit knows no bounds. Victoria embodies the essence of fortitude, facing life's challenges with unwavering determination and grace. She approaches any hurdle with a steadfast resolve, refusing to succumb to fear and discouragement.

I had the privilege of serving in a strategic forum with her and she wasted no time in notching her position around the board-room table.

As a mother, she single-handled raised and shaped the lives of her children with courage and grace – a testament to her unyielding spirit.

—Zanele Mvelase
Franchisee McDonalds
South Africa.

TABLE OF CONTENTS

INTRODUCTION

There's an old saying, 'Success is when preparedness meets opportunity'. Therefore, success for me is a long-term plan, fuelled by commitment and consistent habits.

I come from humble beginnings and faced many obstacles, such as struggling to afford tertiary tuition, being a single mother, and failing at several business start-ups, before I transformed and worked my way up to become a corporate executive of two of the top four banks in South Africa.

I've always wanted to get into formal business; this has been my dream since I was a kid. My emotional strength enabled me to seize the opportunities presented because I was ready and positioned for it, and then pursued it. My mental strength became a game-changer, opening me up to expectancy.

As an entrepreneur franchisee with iconic global brands, I'm able to represent my community of franchisees at global chairperson councils.

In these roles and functions, I apply the same mindset of growth and expectancy. This has been my attitude towards living a thriving life. Therefore, it is one's own decision and responsibility to choose and influence their life experience. So, choose life and the abundance of it, remembering that life's a journey through valleys and hills. You need a resilient mindset for navigation. Then trust your inner voice, go after your life with all your heart and mind, and watch favour pour over you as the universe conspires to make you victorious.

It worked for me, and it will surely work for you, as this approach is powered by infinite intelligence and the wisdom available to all of us and within us.

In my corporate leadership role as both an executive and entrepreneur, as well as a mother, I've always mentored and inspired those I lead. This has become a passion of mine, and the satisfaction of seeing life-changing results in others through life coaching is amazing. With self-development, continuous improvement, and a curious mindset, I reviewed insights and literature from experts in different fields such as biology, neuroscience, spirituality, psychology, leadership, and business, to empower myself with the knowledge of those who have expanded their knowledge and expertise. This enabled me to come up with a specific model and process. I've also applied these processes with my mentees. This has worked for people who wanted guidance and were committed to bringing about positive and lasting change in their lives. It is now my duty to step up and be their role model and assist with their transformation journey.

People have had enough of being invisible, unheard, overlooked, and abused.

> *'There is no greater agony than bearing an untold story inside you.'*

—MAYA ANGELOU

In my country, South Africa, there's a history of violence—especially towards women and children, even in their own homes—and the victims suffer silently. This is also prevalent in many other societies and countries.

So, this book is really meant to help people who currently face hardships and are struggling to rediscover themselves, connect to their identity, and find purpose in their lives.

Through inspirational experiences and actionable techniques, they can reframe their reality, go after their dreams, and lead purposeful lives.

Let's get started on building your resilience to face the challenges life throws at you, and pursue your desires with the determination that's required to achieve them.

1

BEGIN WITH AN END IN MIND

What Are You Telling Yourself?

'All achievements, all earned riches,
have their beginnings in an idea.'

—Andrew Carnegie

I was a young, ambitious kid who dreamed of owning a mansion and a big business; this was inspired by what I saw when my father took me to visit some of the Cape Town suburbs in apartheid South Africa at the time. I started out as a confident, bold, and fearless child, and I had a seat at the table as an eleven-year-old with these big dreams. This was because my father, fondly called 'The Boss' by everyone, was the pillar of my strength. He was my coach and mentor, and he poured life wisdom into me. He also instilled a love of reading in me. Well, this was better than washing dishes and doing house chores. I think my entrepreneurial and leadership spirit was planted during this phase in my life. While other girl-children were playing house, I was at the adult seat, playing card games for money. Of course, my mom was against this, but my father defended this by saying, 'Cards will teach her to think and have a life strategy'. At the time, this was all lost to me and my understanding.

I'd go to the gym for professional boxers and assist my dad there; I was a gym runner who had the menial tasks of bringing water and carrying buckets, bandages, and skipping ropes. I was a curious child full of zest and interest in life. At that young age, I did my first trade. I negotiated with Dad's jeweller friend to give me a few watches to sell for him. Little did I know that this was called consignment. I would take products to sell on his behalf and make a profit. I understood what it meant to buy and sell, and that's when I caught the bug of business.

It may sound far-fetched, but I was taught to drive cars despite my young age. Yes, I drove real cars at eleven years old. Well, it started with me parking cars, washing them, and being kind of a valet service kid. In my father's eyes, I was a trustworthy kid with the potential to do more. Because I was a curious child, it was easy for me to be taught. My imagination and creativity were activated and welcomed.

During my growing up years under the apartheid system, I was my father's constant companion, and I was exposed to insightful information and conversed with the best minds of the day.

It was like a 'take a girl-child to work' type of thing. That's how I got a seat at the table. Amidst the worst political times in South Africa, I had a colourful and enchanted childhood.

Tough times build character

When tragedy hit my family, I was deeply affected. My father passed away from a sudden illness. I was only thirteen years old. Grief grabbed me and tied me up in knots; I felt lost and invisible. I had no voice.

Cultural dynamics don't allow children to be visible during death and grieving time. It was just for adults, as if children felt no grief. Trauma set in and was turned inwards.

I was aware of the pain that the adults felt, but I, too, as a child, felt it intensely.

Because my father was my anchor. And now he was gone. I drifted away and had no direction in my life for a while.

I sit here and look back, reflecting on how far I've come as an independent and resilient woman and entrepreneur who made choices to rise from the darkness that consumed me after the loss of my father.

As an adolescent who was gripped by unresolved grief and was unsupported emotionally at home, I became vulnerable to others.

I was naively drawn into a relationship built on infatuation, and my choices ended up in teenage pregnancy. I went from a bad situation to a worse one within a few years. The darkness of shame and condemnation grew. Cultural stereotypes and judgements suffocated me. I was on autopilot for most of my youth and early adulthood.

The only choice I thought I had was to marry the father of my child to right the situation I'd put myself in. Of course, getting married at a young age without even understanding who I was and what I wanted in life was never going to work out well. I recall not having a wedding or a celebration. I used to say to my friends at the time in jest, 'I woke up and I was married'. I can't even recall the answer I gave to the judge who married us in court. It was every inch a shotgun marriage, as it was quick and didn't have much preparation. It didn't even involve my own family.

So, I can't recall whether I said 'I do', 'I can', or 'I will' in my response to the vows. It was a blur, and those five minutes passed very quickly. That's the vulnerability I'm referring to. Don't get me wrong; I wasn't dragged to the altar or anything like that. My life was on autopilot, though. I was vulnerable to suggestion, as I was knee-deep in the shame I believed I'd brought my family. I compromised my internal beliefs and intuition; I'll share more on this later.

I made one bad choice after another as I tried to rely on a relationship built on an unstable foundation. I then stayed longer in the relationship for all the wrong reasons. For the kids, for the dog, for the house that I built, and most importantly at the time, because I wondered who I'd be if I lost this identity. At least I had a role as a mother and a wife. So many people in relationships that don't work are imprisoned by their own fears, as I was. Are you? So, I put up with an abusive relationship because I was afraid to admit failure once again and bring my family more shame. I endured the hardships. But with grace, I finally took charge of my life and my own story.

Stepping up took courage

Piercing through your own glass ceiling of pain comes from crucible moments that have life-changing impact. In my case,

I was feeling overwhelmed with abuse—physical abuse which pushed me to the edge, making me ready to throw in the towel of my own life. This is one of the key reasons I wrote this book.

I ended up in hospital following an abusive event. It was a sobering moment when a doctor had an earnest chat with me in the hospital after I'd regained consciousness. That doctor touched my soul in that conversation. Angels come in many forms; the doctor was one of them for me. I'll expand on this in the coming chapters.

It was year's end when I left the hospital, with everyone in a festive and jolly mood. Meanwhile, I pondered who I was and what I'd become. Added to this was the fact that I was now being referred to psychiatry for assistance due to depression.

Soon after this, precisely on the first day of the new year, my mom and I attended the funeral of a young man we knew who'd tragically lost his life. While there, something challenged me and shifted my perspective. So, in our culture, women don't go to the cemetery if the deceased died a tragic death. They stay home, and only men go to do the burial. While waiting, women pray, sing, and console each other. A young lady in her early twenties stood up to address us at this funeral gathering of women and she stirred my spirit to the core. She finished by giving those who carried a burden, and felt they had no way out, some guided instructions to try at home. I felt that was directed at me, and took up the challenge. Another angel had appeared to me in the form of this young lady.

To get out of a bad place, mentally and physically, I had to choose a life and actions that would ensure I thrive. Through faith, self-development, self-discovery, studying, and seizing business opportunities, I slowly regained my inner strength and mental resilience. I could breathe, and I was filled with the belief that I had the capacity to change my life. *If you're trying to put up and be normal,* as Maya Angelou says, *you'll never know how amazing you are.*

Finding me

My journey of self-discovery led me to ask myself the question:

Who are you and what do you want?

With the past behind me, and armed with the answer to my question and mental toughness, I knew that I was the master of my life story and the captain of my soul. I was self-reliant and liberated. My confidence and courage grew. I became curious and was excited that I knew where to start. All my skills and education, as well as that eleven-year-old mindset programming, came in to assist me in executing my personal and professional transformation.

This spurred me to rediscover my inner strength to navigate life and be prepared for whatever it threw at me. I had the freedom and absence of fear to pursue my dreams with intensity and determination. So, I began to do the things I loved and wanted to do. I travelled the world, which opened my mind to developing a growth mindset and an appreciation of creation.

What I figured in the pursuit of my dreams is that *my state of mind determines the quality of my life.*

Ask yourself like I did: Are you stuck? Are you overwhelmed, burdened, and/or defeated by your circumstances? Are your self-limiting beliefs the chains dragging you down?

Don't despair. You, too, can change your life by taking charge of your life story.

We all have an innate strength within us; this is our gift. First, we must accept this innate strength, and cultivate and harness the mind. To draw on this strength really depends on each individual and their chosen state of mind. Success requires 'success consciousness'. Find a quality role model, as I was inspired by many others in my life experiences as well.

I draw from my own life experiences of undergoing hardships, which took me to a dark place mentally and caused me to suffer emotionally and act out behaviourally. I made choices in a state of fear, failure, and self-limiting beliefs.

I must tell you, though, that no number of self-help books will make a choice for you to take action to 'transform' your life. *Ultimately, you must decide who you are and what you want—and be committed to it.* Then, you must be convinced about your idea and have an unshakeable desire. With your belief in and determination about your idea, create a plan; then, start with small executable goals to create quality habits. This will boost your confidence and competencies as you gain one win after the next.

I'm so blessed and grateful now for the crucible moments I experienced, because they stirred my mind then. They caused me to pause and reflect, giving me the courage to start the journey to self-transformation.

The power of thoughts

It all began when I understood that my thoughts were powerful enough to deliver my dreams. I had to reprogramme my subconscious memories and the self-limiting stories I was telling myself. I had to replace them with courage, confidence, and certainty in my abilities. I had to act on the things I desired with determination.

Over the years, my growth mindset positioned me well for achieving personal goals, including successfully completing a Bachelor of Arts degree in psychology, a Master of Business Administration (MBA), and many other executive programmes. I was obsessed with investing in myself, as I understood that being on autopilot meant I wasn't taking care of the most important person—me. My executive business coach, Brian Kanyangarara, used to say to me, 'Take care of number one first, and then you can be there for others'.

Practical tips for everyday life

- Because I was a curious child, it made it easy for me to be taught.
- There's an old saying, 'Success is when preparedness meets opportunity'.
- Piercing your own glass ceiling of pain comes from crucible moments that have life-changing impacts.

- None of the self-help books you read will make a choice for you. Ultimately, you must decide who you are and what you want. Then, you must be convinced about your idea and have the unshakeable desire to pursue it.
- My mental strength became a game-changer, opening me up for expectancy.

2

HELLO, HOLY YOU

Rising to Meet Your Truest Self

*'If one has courage, nothing can dim the light
which shines from within.'*

—MAYA ANGELOU

It wasn't smooth sailing for the communities of the dusty township of Langa, Cape Town, South Africa, being under the apartheid regime. But from my childhood perspective, I had an enchanted and colourful adolescence amid the storm of apartheid. Because I had a great role model in my dad, I experienced many instances and applications of real-world wisdom. And just as suddenly, he was gone, and I lost my way; I fell into a depressed state.

I had to dig deep within my soul to overcome the hardship of my youth. With passion and obsession, I searched for who I was at the core in order to figure out the purpose of my life. And in the process, I stumbled on a recipe for successful transformation.

It was my identity reset to my authentic self. It was love, an infinite intelligence, and infinite wisdom within me. This enabled me to navigate my way to a better self to reclaim my life and find meaning.

In this rediscovery journey, I stayed true to my soul and managed to rise to become a franchisee owner of an iconic global brand, McDonald's. However, my path was not at all linear. It was multidimensional and fraught with hardships, depression, and some pockets of wins. With the inner strength and constant overcoming of each battle I found myself in, I progressed. I moved forward with mental resilience.

Lesson 1: Digging deep within

By the end of this book, you'll have arrived at an understanding of and belief in your inner strength, as I did mine. Through my experiences of accessing and harnessing my strength to overcome hardships, you'll get a glimpse of what's needed to develop your inner strength. We all possess this inner strength, but we often don't recognise it. I unconsciously dimmed my own light and let others take the lead. To brighten this light takes time, and I'll share steps on how you, too, can work towards shining the light within. Also, the lessons from my failures, and how a person can become derailed by their thoughts and beliefs, are key roadmaps to finding a way out. Even the detours we experience in our lives are sometimes meant to teach us about our own strength and a way to our own purpose.

Through the next few chapters, you'll come to understand that we're designed to handle stress and respond well to it. Sometimes, this is what fuels us to do better. You'll catch a glimpse of the infinite possibilities available to us when we don't give up on ourselves. You'll learn how stress is an alert mechanism for us to become conscious of our physical and environmental states—the body's fight-flight response. However, prolonged stress exposure without emotional support becomes toxic and debilitating.

I came to understand and appreciate that I'm never alone. I have an unseen guide, my higher self. I believe this is a gift from my creator, the divine within me.

This could be called the Universe, Cosmos, Ancestors, the Deity, or even the higher power; *it is my belief that it's within all of us and within each of us.*

This is what inspired me to take the initiative to change my situation. With big dreams and some good seeds sown into my young life, I was ready to change for the better. There will be opportunities you must be primed to notice; these are the changes that will lead to your transformation.

In hindsight, it seemed my adolescent period was a garden of the school of life. I believe it was meant to toughen me mentally for life's valleys and peaks. I had to become resilience-conscious to overcome my hardships.

My father's teachings were insights that were poured into me in my adolescent years, and those lessons came in handy later to guide me into adulthood when I really had no compass to find my way back.

I'll share the learnings that led to positive talks, a belief in myself, and a sense of belonging and being worthy.

Hardships are real, unbearable, or unpleasant situations that can be caused by external factors and have an emotional impact. We've all experienced them in some form, some more deeply and over a longer period than others. My own experience of hardship showed itself when I lost my father suddenly at thirteen years old, and was consumed with unimaginable grief. It was hard to bear. I shut down emotionally and fear hijacked me and took a foothold in my soul.

Every person has experienced a form of pain that traps them in a loop of habitual negativity. This leads us to lose our freedom, and our authentic selves in the process. For me, it was the loss of a loved one and grief that led me to depression.

Lesson 2: Information overload

We possess innate strength, but we don't always know this. We haven't learned how to harness this trait to serve us well in the journey of life.

Here's a real question to consider. How are you going to tap into your innate strength? It's a journey of self-exploration. We may be inundated by visual images and a constant flow of information from various sources, coming at us fast and furious. Our minds are overcrowded by the inputs. With the digital age giving us access to information at our fingertips, this can overwhelm our thoughts and emotions, becoming chaotic to manage if we're not well-equipped.

In the coming chapters, I share how we can keep focusing on our own goals, overcome obstacles, and learn to develop beliefs that will strengthen our resolve in facing challenges head-on.

With this understanding, you'll be better positioned to take full responsibility for your thoughts, beliefs, and choices, and proactively control your actions.

As it is today, my life is the sum of all my thoughts, beliefs, and emotions. As I act or react to these, I forge a certain path for myself.

The environment is a great part of this mix, and its impact can't be underestimated.

I learned how to choose which aspects to impress from my conscious mind to my subconscious one. Ponder that for a moment, as well as how your life has evolved.

> *'In all you're getting, get understanding;*
> *wisdom is the principal thing.'*
>
> —PROVERBS 4:7 (PARAPHRASED)

Lesson 3: Search for meaning

Discovering your identity matters in connecting to your authentic self, essence, and that resilient self that everyone possesses; only then can you champion your dreams.

By rediscovering my identity, I was able to rebuild my life with purpose and live in contentment with my choices without regret. I was clear on what my life should look like, and I faced my past with compassion for myself and others who I believed had brought me harm. I had to take responsibility for myself, my decisions, and my choices. I chose to forgive and let go as a means of freeing myself from the grip of fear and failure.

I was a leader in many fields, roles, and responsibilities— but I was never a leader to myself, which started me on a quest to discover who I was.

In the coming chapters, you'll learn how I dissected and approached this process.

I was intentional about resolving the question, 'Who are you?', and the journey took a life of its own; it took me down many roads I wouldn't have particularly taken. One was a spiritual quest that I embarked on which led me to figure out my own identity. That was the foundation of my dynamic perspective shift, which gave me the ability to look at my life's direction critically. I went on a quest to understand my thoughts, this conscious and subconscious mind, and how they relate to my day-to-day life. Also, I wanted to know how powerful my thoughts are to create my reality. I became aware of and understood all the cultural and social biases and misconceptions about who we are and what society has decided we can be. All those self-limiting beliefs and misconceptions had become a trap.

Lesson 4: Mental resilience

With both science and spirituality as pillars, I managed to rise out of my quest with an understanding that I was stronger than I was giving myself credit for and that I had innate resilience that has always been there. I believe resilience is the key to building innate courage.

What is resilience?

It's the process and outcome of successfully adapting to difficult challenging life experiences, especially through mental, emotional, behavioural flexibility and adjustment to external and internal demands (APA Dictionary of Psychology).

My father was the key to unlocking my resilience. I connected back to my childlike faith and the programming I'd had when I was eleven years old. At that age, I had the bravery and courage to explore fearlessly, knowing I was guided and supported.

Later, I realised that I needed to replace the familiar negative inner dialogue with unfamiliar positive self-talk to impact my day-to-day life in order to bounce back.

You, too, can bounce back from any adversity that you're experiencing now, because you've already overcome some hardships at some point in your life.

This means you and I are *already* resilient, even if we're unconscious of it. The goal is to discover how to let go of the residual impact of the burden of experiences, the hurt that still lives in all of us. The world triggers us, and we react from the memories of experiences; they're embedded in our physiology.

Resilience is a journey; one must be intentional about this pursuit. It's an awareness to stop and realise that you want more goodness out of life, and believe you deserve it. This is the mindfulness that pushes you to seek transformation for a better-quality life.

Lesson 5: Sustaining the identity

I'd made prior changes in my life, but they didn't seem to stick. I usually found myself back in the same place of emotional pitfalls. Why? Simply because I hadn't reprogrammed my self-talk to align with my identity and desires.

A clear and well-defined identity is the crucial piece that leads to a deep connection with your sustained resilience, consistency of application, and positive outlook.

When I reconnected with my inner resilience, it was a do-over. I absorbed the eleven-year-old powerhouse of resilience in my adult years. I was going for the long haul, resolute that I wouldn't take no for an answer. I was excited and optimistic, and understood that the battle was in my mind. I realised that I had a sound mind *(a balanced mind and ability to discern)*, and I needed to exercise this mental capacity. My mental strength was always there in whatever I encountered in life. It was a question of how I was accessing and using it. Consider the same for yourself.

Lesson 6: The building blocks of resilience

To undergo a positive, long-lasting transformation, I needed to have a very compelling *what* and *why*. When I was clear on the *why*, I wanted to change my life. When the *what* became clear, there was a meaning attached to it.

This perspective was reinforced by reading what science shares about how our minds and beliefs influence us. Another view was what spirituality claims of the universe's intention for us. These two forces, science and spirituality, beautifully explain how our sub-conscious mind rules our behaviour. This gave me a compelling enough reason to understand that this can't be a coincidence.

We all know science conducts tests, peer reviews, and research to provide evidence to prove theories and so on. Experts are constantly sharing updates on their search for the purpose of human-kind and all interactions. All evidence points towards the fact that we are what we think, and there's great depth in what *we believe and how it influences our thoughts and behaviours.*

Through neuroscience, we also know that our thoughts in turn influence our emotions, actions, and destiny.

In my rediscovery journey, I had to fall back on the competencies that I discovered over time. One of my tools was a SWOT analysis of myself. It's the ideal way to achieve self-awareness and gives you a better understanding about yourself. Self-improvement begins with a snapshot of your present self, which then helps you work out the gaps on the road to your goals.

It's easy to do a SWOT analysis for a company or a business, but it's harder to do it on yourself. So, I challenge you. Do a personal analysis and have three criteria answered in each quadrant, starting with your weaknesses and ending with your strengths. I'll expand on the personal SWOT analysis in the upcoming chapters.

What's your strength relative to you, your family, and your career or business? Do this for each quadrant. You'll find it to be an interesting analysis, and the outcome might surprise you. This is very useful for you; it's important to start with your own self-development, your own investment into yourself, because I believe we're assets. And if we're going to produce any prosperity in our lives, it must start with some commitment to improving our own selves before we can do so to others.

Another guideline from my toolbox in my self-improvement journey was the Five Cs.

Find *clarity* of direction. Where are you going, and where are you at this point in time? Be specific and concise with the intended direction.

Have a *compelling* reason that moves you. This is an emotion and belief that drives you beyond reasoning.

Be *committed* and have lots of passion. To some extent, be obsessive about whatever it is that you're embarking on to be sustainable.

Be *consistent* and *create* habitual patterns that will help to stay the course.

This, together with your identity, uniqueness, and the true essence embedded within you, is a great combination to propel you forward to a meaningful life.

In the next chapter, we'll look through the eyes of the vibrant, confident eleven-year-old, who was unstoppable, who lived in an environment that lacked freedom but was undeterred and had big dreams for her future.

Practical tips for everyday life

- You must first stop and realise that you want more out of life and that you deserve it.
- Realise that resilience is a journey that takes time, and you must be intentional about wanting to change your situation.
- Even the detours experienced in life are sometimes meant to teach something.
- Do a personal SWOT analysis on yourself.
- I had to become resilience-conscious to overcome my hardships.
- Follow the guidelines of the Five Cs.

3

BROWN CHOCOLATE GIRL

My Influencer

*'Each person must live their lives
as a model for others.'*

—Rosa Parks

We all have role models. Have you considered whom yours is? And why?

This is the one person who inspires you, or the one you'd like to emulate and imbibe their positive characteristics and behaviours. I had a few role models in my life. In my adolescence, the most impactful was my father. As his daughter, I looked up to him as someone full of wisdom.

My wise role model

Let me tell you a little bit about my dad, Solomon, affectionately known as The Boss.

My most fond and vivid memory of him is when I was in primary school. I was about nine years old, and walked home from school every afternoon. I was a very petite child; my siblings gave me the nickname of 'soupbones' as one who was skinny. My father used to sit on the porch with his friends, and I'd walk towards the gate of the house. He'd smile and call out when I walked through the gate, 'Ah, there comes my brown chocolate girl'. He'd be beaming, and his friends would look at him, also smiling, probably thinking, 'Oh, man. This guy and his kid!'. But that moment would fill me up from the bottom of my soul to the top of my head with such soothing energy. The feeling of being home was the love that was palpable from him.

It was such a powerful memory that I still cherish and appreciate it to this day. My nickname became *brown chocolate girl,* and the locals would tease me and say, in vernacular, *waza waza, langena ibityo lam,* loosely translated as 'there comes my skinny one'. I didn't like that at all, but Dad would turn it around and say, 'It's a good thing to be slim because you are a queen, as in Queen Victoria'.

That would make me grin. I indeed felt like a queen. Maybe that's why I have tendencies of thinking I'm royalty today—you know, 'African queen vibes!'. My friends fondly call me Queen Vee. Okay, I digress.

Lesson 1: Build positivity in others

My dad had a knack for making everyone smile. I recall how he'd change a negative situation to a positive one. My cousin sister, Linda grew up close to us, and called my father Dad, too. Once, she was teased that she was *Notyatyambo,* meaning flower. But she thought it was a mean word. So, she ran to my dad crying. He embraced her and asked why the tears. She told him that people were mean being to her, and he responded with a smile, 'Oh, that's a special name, because indeed you are a flower'. Linda was complimented as being a beauty; she walked out of there confident, asking us to call her 'flower'. How she cried and afterwards quickly took on the name is a family joke to this day.

My father had a huge personality and was a big influence in my life. In my eyes, there was nothing that my father couldn't do, and he taught me the same attitude. That's the power of a role model in a young mind.

Growing up in a tense political environment caused by apartheid, there was segregation based on racial lines and no political or economic freedom for certain groups. Everybody knew apartheid had been abolished as a human rights violation. But because of the restrictions imposed, people were forced to pull together and form a thriving community that produced scholars, entrepreneurs, sports personalities, and musicians; people learned to hustle. It became a self-contained community. This fostered a network to protect the inner community from perceived threats. My father was instrumental in most of the networks that made our communities vibrant and thriving. Despite the political environment, I grew up in a community whose members were united in what they were doing. There was a sense of camaraderie and a will to overcome. This environment, unjust as it was, toughened people who didn't give up.

Lesson 2: Self-respect is your power

I recall one experience with my father that's still impressed on my mind. It was a visit to the Stellenbosch suburb in the Western Cape. This area is the heart of wealth, winelands, and old money in South Africa. A beautiful countryside, full of vineyards, it produces some of the best wines in the world. I was around eleven years of age and had just returned from school.

As usual, I expected to go with my father wherever he was planning to go. That day, he told me, 'I am going alone today. I have an important meeting'. I was disappointed, but thought he'd said this in front of my other siblings so they would think we weren't going. I snuck into the car and hid myself in the back seat. He didn't realise I was there as he drove out. When he was about twenty minutes or so out in the motorway, I came out of my hiding place. He was not pleasantly surprised at all, and I was scolded. And because he couldn't turn the car around due to time constraints, he continued to drive and warned me to stay in the car because he was attending an important meeting.

We got to Stellenbosch, to what appeared to be a wine farm and an office block. Dad got out and warned me again: 'I want you to stay in the car, I will not be long'. I nodded in reply. It was autumn and still warm weather, so he left the car windows open and gave me the keys. Soon after he left, I thought for a bit. I realised this wasn't the first 'meeting' I'd been to, and thought I wouldn't disturb him. After a few minutes in the car, I exited and confidently entered the building.

I opened the office door. There was a nice white lady in the reception area. We chatted and she asked me who I was and how I came to be there. I responded that my dad had just walked in, but that I wasn't sure which meeting room he'd gone into. Yes, I could converse very easily in English as a kid. The lady walked me into the meeting room. When I entered, I saw the longest wooden table ever; it was the boardroom table. I immediately had bulging eyes.

As a kid, it looked giant. There were white men wearing white shirts and ties seated around it. My dad was standing at one end of the table. He wore a Dunhill cotton shirt, with sleeves rolled up to below his elbow, and grey trousers. To me, he always looked dapper in anything he wore, even in smart casual dress.

Everyone in the room turned to look when I entered, escorted by the receptionist. I'd interrupted my father, who was speaking at the time. He looked at me and paused, then without missing a beat, he said, 'Gentlemen this is my daughter, Victoria. She was supposed to sit in the car,' giving me a stern look.

Everyone was welcoming. They were super nice and smiled at me with 'hellos'. They said it was okay for me to be in the room, and I could sit there at the table. Wow, that was my first seat at a boardroom table and one that would pave the way to many more.

That day was such a blessing for me as I saw my father in action in his element as a leader and speaking authoritatively.

What struck me the most was how comfortable he was addressing them—the white men—as peers and an equal, not lesser than them. In return, they were comfortable with him and spoke casually with each other; they were even sharing a smoke.

It shattered my misconception of being 'afraid' of white people, which was a common misconception in our community. On our way home, puzzled, I asked him, 'Are you not afraid of them?'. He looked at me with a firm 'no'. He clearly didn't understand why I thought that way.

I then said, 'I hear they don't like black people'.

He responded, 'Well, they are the ones afraid of us, and that is why they are like that'. He seemed deep in thought and finally said, 'Fear is dangerous; you know wars have been started out of fear'.

I didn't get it at the time, but many years later. I understood his words. He further said, 'They are the same as us. They are just people and not super-people. They just have a different skin colour'.

From that time on, I saw everyone as equal, irrespective of their race or colour.

Lesson 3: Build strength through community spirit

It was lovely to grow up in that community, despite the circumstances of politics. We had facilities such as well-stocked libraries, halls for sports and music, and swimming facilities. We kids were active with all these initiatives for children's upliftment and enjoyment. I recall being the secretary of the youth club at the age of twelve.

Years later, the Community Centre celebrated a milestone, and I was invited. I was surprised and impressed to see my handwriting in some of the minutes of the youth club. I'd written very legibly as a young person, and my handwriting was preserved in the records. That's the spirit of the community I grew up in. My father encouraged us to learn to swim. My older brother had swimming as part of his training routine, and I was always in the water. Between the ages of nine and thirteen, I swam in competitions. There was a culture of learning, as education was seen as a great equaliser and a push for emancipation.

Lesson 4: Generosity and kindness

Another aspect that intrigued me about my dad was his willingness to meet people night or day. There were people coming in every other day to see him, whether it was to ask for advice for sports coaching, for entrepreneurial reasons, or regarding a community issue. Our front door was forever open, a literal 'open door policy'. People came in for all sorts of assistance, and they'd say, 'We're here to see The Boss'.

Yes, that was my dad. He was fondly called The Boss. We had a small three-room house. The front of the house was almost like an open-plan dining–lounge room and kitchen. One room was what we now call the TV lounge area. Then, it was called the 'sitting room'. And my father used to see visitors in the sitting room; it was a quiet part of the house. While he consulted with the visitors, my duty was to make the tea and coffee. I was the only kid always in the house around my dad. All my other siblings were out on the street, playing and having fun.

Being home, I was the one to make the tea any time Dad said, 'Hey, can we have a cup of tea please?'. My mom, of course, would help me in the kitchen to set it up and make it look nice, but carrying and serving it was my duty. After serving the tea, I'd quietly sit at the foot of my father, watching TV with the volume turned all the way down. I got to eavesdrop and observe how my father engaged the visitors who were looking for assistance of all sorts. I'd listen to what was said, pretending to be watching the TV.

As a curious kid, I stayed close to my dad when kids weren't allowed to sit or listen to adult talk. He was fine with me being there.

A regular visitor I enjoyed was another young coach, Monde Sibaca, who trained his own brother, Bashew Sibaca. He came to talk to my father about boxing matters, and that's how I got to know my father was sharing his knowledge with others, too. Monde would often have a hearty laugh at my father's use of humour in coaching.

One time a lady, all dressed in black, came to visit my father. I later understood that she was a widower and needed help with an eviction notice. She was also a housewife, and her husband had been the provider. My father said, 'No, don't worry, I'll sort it out'. When she left, my father called someone to find out about the local housing office and told them what was happening, asking why she was being evicted.

Guess what? My father took care of it. The lady returned a few weeks later to thank my father with a gift of baked scones. Because I was there to make tea, I got to sample the scones before the other kids.

It appeared that her situation was resolved, and it was an smiles around. That was my father in a nutshell. He was such a kind, generous, and loving person.

Lesson 5: There's more than one way to acknowledge God

My father was well-respected and well-received by the community. And yet, oddly, he never went to church. Well, let me correct that. When I was a kid, I never saw him go to church. We all went to church as a family; my mom mostly led the troop and my dad, well, he was the one left behind. I used to joke and say to him, 'Are you not coming to church with us?'.

And he would say, 'No, God already knows me. You guys go and speak to God for yourselves'.

People used to laugh about that and joke, 'Ah, Boss doesn't go to church?'.

Interestingly, it turned out that the church leadership knew my dad. As children we attended Sunday School, and before the service started, a deacon would call out to me, 'Quickly run and go ask your father and ask for that thing'.

And I'd be like, 'What is the thing I must ask for?'.

And they would say to me, 'Tell your father that they need that thing; he knows what it is we are asking for'.

I'd run back home, which wasn't far from the church. And I'd share that I got this funny message. I'd relay to my dad that the church was asking for the 'thing'. And my father wouldn't be surprised or ask me to clarify. But he would signal Uncle Tse, our neighbour and long-time driver, to sort this out and drive me back to church. He'd get up and pick up a box in the back room, then say, 'Come, do you want to go back to church?'.

And I'd sometimes say yes, sometimes no. He'd go and deliver this box to the church. Over time, I learned that my father was giving them the special church wine, which he kept stock of in case they ran out. If they didn't manage their stock well, they knew that the only person who could help them out of the sticky situation was The Boss.

I guess when my father answered 'I know God' when asked why he didn't go to church, he meant it in his own way. I always thought that was funny—but in hindsight, there's more than one way of knowing God and praising Him in one's life. I think my dad was on to something, as his heart was full of goodness, kindness, and generosity. *To him, God was everywhere and not just in church. I'd come to learn this much later in my life as an adult.*

Lesson 6: Family

My siblings all got the same love and attention. My sister Maureen, whom I came into this world immediately after, always said that I was Dad's favourite. Meanwhile, I thought my older brother was the favourite. This sibling debate about favourites went on for years. We would compare notes, such that I was taught to drive earlier than her. She drove at sixteen, but never got interested after learning. She knew how to play cards and went horse racing with us a few times. But she just wasn't into it at all; she loved her friends in the neighbourhood. And she was a popular beauty as well. This was true for all my siblings. My four older sisters were all stunning beauties, and I was always fascinated watching them doll up to go out, or to nice events. They had a busy social life. One of the things I envied about them was that they were studying in faraway boarding schools. This seemed so cool, having to board trains, buy clothes, and seemingly live an independent life away from home. But my dad would hear none of it for me; he kept me close.

Well, Maureen would always tell me, 'You owe me, Victoria, as I used to wash dishes while you played cards, went to gym, did homework'.

I'd argue right back, 'But you weren't keen on any of that'.

And she'd say, 'You were favoured and taught more than me'.

I ended up having to pay up in some form. I call it 'sibling tax', which I'm happy to provide my big sister with, because I love her, and she's a strong, caring person. I guess we all respond differently to environmental input, but as the last born in the family, my father just kept me closer. I was open to listen, observe, and learn from my dad.

Lesson 7: Negotiation 101

Nothing was impossible for me at that time, as my sheer will was in full force. I'd negotiate for everything as Dad taught me. I remember my first stint as an entrepreneur. My father would go out and meet all these interesting people from various backgrounds outside our community, and I was usually in tow.

One time, he went to visit his friend, a jewellery store owner in the nearby suburb of Mowbray. Whilst my dad was busy talking, I'd be admiring the jewellery on display. Everything looked beautiful and shiny and expensive, especially the rings.

But the watches caught my attention. I thought I could sell these in my 'hood. I was *certain* they would sell. I'd seen and heard people talking about and admiring watches. Their beauty and status were attached to these objects. As we were leaving, I had the courage to say, 'I like this watch'.

My father said, 'Oh, do you like it? I can get it for you. Do you want it?'.

I said, 'No, I don't want it for me. I want to sell them. Can I sell them?'. My father and his friend smiled at each other. They asked me a few questions about my plan. We talked price and decided that I should sell at a discount so I could make quick sales. The discount thing I heard from Dad many times. I convinced the jeweller, and he agreed to give me three watches. Obviously, I got the watches without paying for them. *Maybe my dad stood for surety or paid for them. I don't know, but I got them.* It was on consignment, as I understood it later. I sold the watches in two days to the people who came to my father's house. And suddenly, I had new orders, and I sold more. I got mine later without payment as a commission for selling and made some money. I was hustling when I was a kid. I would sell anything I could get my hands on that I believed would make profit. That was one of my earliest encounters with money, my relationship with it, and my understanding of it.

My father was a pillar of strength and a great cheerleader. It didn't matter to him that I was his youngest child; he seemed to know I'd learn the most from him. His actions were my best teachers. I had the ringside seat to gather his wisdom.

Practical tips for everyday life

- Consider who's your role model, and why.
- Come to a resolution without fear. 'Fear is dangerous; you know wars have been started out of fear.'
- Education is a great equaliser and a force for emancipation.
- To my father, God was everywhere and not just in church.
- Your goodness need not be restricted to the house of God.

4

CRUCIBLE CHILDHOOD

Seeds of Positive Self-talk

Life itself is the most wonderful fairy-tale.

— Hans Christian Anderson

Ever wonder where your self-talk, positive or negative, stems from? And who or what influenced it the most? Very often, it's from childhood conditioning. In my case, it was my father who had the most impact on my self-talk. It was through my interactions with him that I picked up much of my soft skills. However, the most important thing is the chatter we have with ourselves. I was a curious kid, and my dad never tired of my inquisitive mind. My questions were never dismissed or sidelined. That laid the foundation to bounce back to a positive outlook on life.

Lesson 1: Ringside learning of mental fitness

Entertainment and sports were the highlights for everyone in our community. People needed an outlet from the social oppression. Some of the activities were boxing, music, and cricket, with leisure activities being huge social events. My father had his hand in most of them. In the sports fraternity, he was a boxing promoter and a coach, as well as an entrepreneur. My older brother was a boxing champion. I grew up in a household that took sports very seriously. And this is where I learned a lot of stuff about leadership, commitment, communication, and coaching.

At the time, I didn't know I was picking up those traits or learning very insightful skills that would serve me well later in life. We'd spend many quality hours hanging out, and he'd tell me wise words that would later bring back memories of who he was, and how he impacted my life.

Once, he said to me, 'Champions are made and not born, and talent alone is not enough'. In hindsight, I realised he always said these statements when he was either at the gym during an intense coaching session or at an event like a boxers' weigh-in on the day of the match. At these events, he would talk about the boxer's odds of winning a match, and always said that it came down to their mental fitness over their physical fitness. He used to say that the latter is easy for any boxer, but it's mental fitness that separates champions from winners.

That was a lesson in mental resilience taught to me right there at an early age.

This nugget of wisdom was sown into me without me even realising; it was an unconscious process. I watched boxers train, particularly my brother, Sydney Hoho. I watched him being coached to become the South African champion in the light-weight and middleweight division. From what I discovered, boxers are resilient sportsmen, as they can bounce back from losing. This is their greatest trait.

Lesson 2: Win or lose? Dust yourself off

Every day, I witnessed discipline and consistency in action, the habits of getting up at five in the mornings for runs and intense evening training sessions. In the community, there was another champion, Bashew Sibaca, a local who was a featherweight champion at the time. At that time, boxing was a big deal, as it was the means of elevating one's social and financial position. Because I spent so much time around my dad at the gym, I watched his coaching style. That allowed me to learn from him in his natural environment.

One's state of mind was always important to my father. During and even after training sessions, my father would advise my brother, 'You have to be aware of what you want, and your heart and mind must be a hundred per cent in it'. He'd guide him to reflect on their winning strategy. Once, my brother lost a fight to a boxing legend called 'Tap-tap Makhathini', and my father said that the loss was a lesson to prepare better for the next fight. He'd repeatedly say to Sydney, 'You are the champ' and 'You are the destroyer'. These remarks were like affirmations in the training session. These words were meant to sink into his unconscious mind and work their power under the surface.

There was an energy of victory in the gym; the focus wasn't on the losing itself, but on the next win. We all believed this.

Sydney was a kind and soft-spoken guy. He wasn't fazed by being a champion, and it didn't go to his head. He was very grounded. I witnessed this man turn from a regular boxer and rise very quickly to the championship level. He earned himself the boxing name *The Young Destroyer*.

He went on to beat the legendary Makhathini in two consecutive rematches at different weight levels. As a result, Makhathini suffered his first professional loss to my brother. The secret was my father's teachings: the mental toughness and belief in beating his opponent was greater than physical fitness.

As the apartheid segregation in sports loosened up, my brother challenged for the white South African title and won against champion Kosie Smith. This was a great achievement for my father, as it was a non-racial title. He bragged about this all the time, saying, 'You see *ntwana,* you must never leave the decision to the judges; it must be an undisputed decision'. Sydney went on to win with a knockout.

These were powerful learning moments. I observed failure embraced as a lesson to improve, not discouragement, and a resilient mindset of conquering one's own fears. That is the stuff resilience is made of—the ability to dust yourself off and keep moving with determination.

Lesson 3: Champions are made, not born

I was between the ages of ten and thirteen when I started learning about state of mind and visualisation, that of seeing and feeling the victory. This was also about leadership indirectly, and I learned that champions are made through coaching. The talent, commitment, and determination of the person coached is sculpted by the trainer. In those moments of training, I was like a sponge absorbing everything I heard my father, the coach, say and do. I also had this victory language embedded in me like a chant. It was information that was downloaded and stayed with me.

I remember us talking about champions during our many drives.

Once, my father declined a prospective boxer, and I asked him why. He responded that he didn't want a boxer with only potential, but with the commitment and heart to go at it. He further explained, using racehorses as a metaphor. He said that racehorses can be great stallions, well-trained and groomed, but the *jockey* is the one that makes the difference.

Confused, I replied, 'But all the jockeys look the same'. They looked like children because they were so short and petite. 'Why do you always choose that horse or that rider?'

And my father would say mysteriously, 'It's never only about the horse'.

His favourite jockey was Garth Puller. At the time of writing, Mr Puller is 72 years old, an ex-jockey and champion trainer (www.sportingpost.co.za).

My father would say, 'Every time Garth Puller gets onto any horse, he can make a horse get into the first three-placement win—and that's a champion'.

He emphasised that it's not about the horse only, and that the jockey's determination, behaviour, and weight on the day also mattered. 'The jockeys are there to direct, guide, and lead the horses, making sure they're consistent in pushing them to the win. So, you always bet on the jockey *and* horse. Garth knows how to handle and push a horse to a win.' I realised this was what my father did back at the gym, coaching boxers to focus on the win. I kept these words to myself. These were the seedlings planted in the fertile young mind.

Lesson 4: Be the self-promoter of your goals

That lesson came in handy when I began my entrepreneurial journey and sought funding from the banks. When I had to support my business plan, I was of the mindset that I was the jockey to any business venture (*the horse*) that I undertook. I was there to guide and direct it to produce value with all the resources at my disposal.

One of the things I learned was how much effort you had to invest in order to get the results that you wanted, because *'Faith without works is dead'*. In hindsight, when I got older, these lessons showed that any outcome was proportional to the effort, consistency, and commitment you put in. Whether it was in studying, relationships, career, new business projects, or getting into the boxing ring, you gain the results of your efforts.

As a result of my regular trips to the gym and training with my father, part of who I am was moulded during this phase.

It happened unconsciously, but part of my positive self-talk is rooted in what my father told me daily at home or the gym. I was programmable and impressionable. To this end, I'm very careful what I say and how I speak to my children, both when they were young, and now as young adults. I often hear parents and teachers use harsh words when disciplining children and young adults. I hear words like, 'You are useless', or 'You will amount to nothing', or 'You are stupid'.

Words are powerful seeds in young minds, and they can break or build up children's self-esteem and confidence.

What kind of words are you using when you speak to the young minds around you?

Consider the seeds of self-talk you're planting. Is it what you want for them?

Lesson 5: Learning through play

Another thing that I learned from this beautiful time in my life was playing cards. It's something that happens even today when I go back to the *ekasi* (a slang word for a township). Elders who know me always say to me, 'This is brown chocolate girl—this kid used to smack us while playing cards. We are not surprised you became an entrepreneur'.

The one thing that used to test my mother's patience was the card games with Dad. My father used to play a game called Rummy. There are fifty-two cards in a single pack, and this was a seven-card game with a maximum of four players. My father taught us all as kids. But I was the one who was most curious and wanted to learn more. I'd come back from school. He'd be sitting at the table, and I'd do my homework quickly. After I finished, he'd teach me Rummy.

He'd say, 'So if you're holding this set of cards, this or that will happen. Think about this scenario'. He was teaching me strategic thinking, which later became a handy tool to navigate through many obstacles. We had this thing working in sync between the two of us.

My father and I had a strategy when playing card games against his friends. The strategy was to intimidate or distract them with my presence as a kid playing a serious game. The hustle was that if I was on form and had a good hand, then I'd play all out and win. If I wasn't, I'd play defence. They would hold all the opponent cards they needed and by reading the game, we could start over. I loved playing the game as it was intriguing, complex, and competitive; it required being sharp, focused, and alert to non-verbal cues. As I learned something from each round of play, it gave me a thrill, win or lose.

From the minute the first player picks up or drops a card, you start to focus, read the cards, and make educated guesses. You start to deduce who's holding what, and decide on your type of play based on the hand you're dealt.

Card games taught me to anticipate people's moves and gave me the ability to 'read the room'. Out of this game, in hindsight, I understood life strategy through card games.

A great trait I picked up was not to be a 'sore loser' in my life, which is necessary for a resilient mindset. My relationship with money grew in this period as well. I learned how to value, grow, and save it. I used to say to Dad, 'I will have a big house, like the ones in Camps Bay or Stellenbosch suburb on the beautiful Atlantic seaboard and picturesque winelands of the Western Cape'. This dream came from my exposure to a different way of life through our suburb visits.

He would smile and say, 'Of course, but you have to make money and save it, and then you can do anything you put your mind to'.

I believed this was possible.

My father used to joke, 'As long as you know how to play cards, you'll never be hungry in your life, and you'll never struggle. It will teach you to think of the next move'. I now understand that he meant I could look at my life, think about it, and rework whatever wasn't working out.

Lesson 6: Confidence builder

Every time I tried something new, Dad encouraged me with 'You can do it'. Sometimes, he would remind me of what I'd last achieved. He'd encourage me even if I failed, saying I had to practice some more. Being supported gave me motivation and a boost in self-confidence. When you lose money in a card game, other people freak out, but my father was very calm about it. I would be thinking, 'OMG, will I be allowed to play again?'. But Dad was cool about it, making excuses like, 'It was not our day. You win some and lose some'. And he always said this with a smile. It would be such a relief, and I came to value money differently.

I didn't just play in my father's house. We played in other people's homes that he visited. So, we'd come back late at night to my mother, who wouldn't be impressed. She'd scold him, and my father would be like, 'She's done more work in there than she could do at school'.

On weekends, I'd play in these off-site places and people got to know me. I also got to know them. I got exposed to how other different cultures and races lived, and an expanded mind-set grew from our excursions. This excited me and fuelled my dreams of achieving something different to what I saw in my neighbourhood.

One moment, I was this kid who was playing with their children in their backyard. And the next, my father would say, 'Come, wash your hands and get into the game!' and I'd switch immediately. The next minute, I'd be sitting at a table playing a serious card game with serious money. This later taught me the ability to compartmentalise roles, which is a crucial requirement for resilience and a success mindset.

This was uncommon for a kid, I must admit, but it was precious and colourful and full of love. It got me a seat at the table where I was heard. I was seen. People had time for me. I felt appreciated. I felt supported and like I belonged.

Lesson 7: Education is a key investment in life

It was always drilled into me that to succeed, 'you've got to study. Education is critical in opening the doors of life'. One highlight of my life was the honour of meeting Tata Nelson Mandela in 1993 at the Ritz Hotel. We were invited to assist in pre-election voter education for 1994's first democratic election campaign in South Africa because of our boxing involvement. He shared his love for boxing with us. We all knew this incredible world-renowned statesman, who also reinforced what my father once said about education—that I had to continue studying, as it unlocked great potential. And that I must ensure I learned as much from white fellow men, because they had a great advantage and head start.

My father would drop me at the library and would tell me, 'I will pick you up later'. That was when my love for books developed. I reckoned it must be a great part of my education, as my father and I would talk about the books I read. The more we discussed, the more passionate I became about books. I read voraciously. Enid Blyton's books were my favourites; the adventures there seemed to emulate my adventurous life at the time. Reading led to curiosity to see the world, and that's when I developed a thirst for travelling. What was modelled for me by my father, I did for my children—reading to them from a young age. It became a family hobby to read. My friends even noticed that I only gave books as birthday gifts.

Lesson 8: Entrepreneurship

My father used to say to look at what people need and take that as an opportunity to find what to sell. 'Be mindful, and don't sell what the other person is already selling. Solve a problem that people are willing to pay for your solution'.

We used to drive past Cape Town station, and would see all these people selling the same fruit by the roadside. And my father would say, 'You see, you can't do business like that. If that one is selling oranges, you can't sell oranges as well. Find another fruit that's in season, and you sell that. At least, give the customer a choice'.

The fundamentals of business were instilled in me early enough. Entrepreneurs solve problems in communities. I later came to appreciate the insightful mentoring from Dad, especially when I studied for my Master of Business Administration.

As a kid, I wasn't aware that my mind was being fed with business strategies, which included learning to identify opportunities, trading skills and risk-taking. Feeling trusted and valued gave a boost to my self-worth and self-esteem. This was stored deep in my memory, and it became useful in turning my life around. There's one thing to say you trust someone, but to show them speaks volumes. Think about who you are to someone. Are you someone else's role model?

Parents have a great first-time influence in a child's life, so consider your words and actions towards them.

In my father's boxing tournaments, I was trusted to be at the ticket sales booth. As a youngster, I was given the role of looking after the cash and counting money. That's how my father saw value in me. Later in my career, it was no wonder I ended up being the Executive of Cash Operations for one of the major banks in the country, Standard Bank. I was responsible for the physical cash value chain, from procuring, distribution, and logistics to storage of cash in both domestic and foreign currencies.

Lesson 9: The power of encouraging young minds

I don't know how many eleven-year-olds drove cars in those days. I learned all about a stick shift car when I was nine or ten years old. I would get into the car, sit in the passenger seat, and view outside to enjoy the ride. My dad would say, 'No, don't look outside. Look here at the gears; look at my feet. Do you know what this is?'. And he'd tell me, 'This is a clutch. This is a brake. This is an accelerator, and this is for fuel'. I soon learned to be observant of road directions and landmarks. He'd check if I was noticing my environment.

Dad would talk me through everything he was doing, and I started becoming an even more curious-minded person. Then, I got into the habit of saying, 'Let me change the gear for you' when he had to change it. I'd press the gear shift from first to second gear and so on. By the time I was eleven years old, I was driving. I was sent to get things from the local deli that was near the house. (I would drive with a licensed person, of course.)

When I was, I think, about twelve to thirteen, I drove in and out of Langa to the nearest suburb to buy beverages, ice, and food at night, with an adult driver. My father had an interesting entertainment lifestyle, and influencers were some of the interesting people he associated with.

My father didn't have a liquor license, but he had what we now know as a members' sports club. There was a great vibe on weekends, with cards played at the round table and others watching sports on TV and chatting about life. But this was only for members and their visitors, very decent folks. My father never drank alcohol, but most of his friends did, and he was okay with that. A stranger couldn't just walk in and mingle with the regulars. It was known to be a strict place; only the *grootman*'s (the ekasi's wise man) patrons were there. I used to run errands driving to the nearest deli or café for ice and take-aways. I later got a nickname: the 'driver kid'.

But the beauty of the gatherings was the wisdom shared by the men and women there. They took particular care in dressing up. They were stylish, and this was my favourite observation. In today's fashion, they would look like they stepped out of any

Mayfair fashion district in London. They looked dapper and had swagger. I grew up seeing luxury brand names like Pall Mall, Crockett & Jones, and Daks. The patrons were business owners, sports leaders, and corporate execs, and came from different neighbourhoods. They would discuss current affairs, whether they involved politics, social issues, sports, or innovation. They loved to brainstorm. Some of them later became pioneers of industries and influential people that I'm proud to have known during that time. Some, like Bra KK and Zithulele Combi, became my role models.

Guess where Victoria was?

I had a seat at the big table, and I learned from these engagements. I got to be seen and felt I was enough. Well, my father did impact how I looked at my life. As his companion, I got to learn from his day-to-day work right there at the ringside. This is where most insights were shared that became the seeds of my mental resilience.

He did influence a lot of my attitude towards life. And I think he deliberately poured insights into me, and shared his wisdom. Maybe he had foresight, and, therefore, mentored me from a young age. I'm grateful for this part of my life that forever shaped me.

Like all good things in life, though, they didn't last.

The storms of life came furiously, sweeping me away from my glorious adolescence to test my resolve in the next phase of my teenage years.

Practical tips for everyday life

- Champions are made and not born. Talent alone is not enough.
- You must be aware of what you want, and your heart and mind must be a hundred percent in it.
- Education is an asset. Invest early on in life.
- Any outcome is proportional to the effort, consistency, and commitment you put in.
- Be a positive role model to young people.

5

TURBULENCE ON AUTOPILOT

Dimming of the Inner Light

'A dead end is just a good place to turn around.'

—NAOMI JUDD

Can you imagine being on an Airbus, 36,000 feet above sea level, and suddenly hitting turbulence, with thunderstorms … and there's no pilot at all in the cockpit?

I can imagine that would be a bumpy and scary ride. I'd never want to be on that kind of a flight. Guess what? From my enchanted, colourful, bright, and loving childhood, I was suddenly thrust into this dark mode, where it felt like I was on a flight that was on autopilot while hitting massive turbulence. And that's how the next part of my young life evolved. From the loss and grief, I was hit with such unimaginable pain that

I couldn't fathom how to deal with it. So, this is my story of how when pain and grief is unmanaged—especially for a child or young adult—it sets off all kinds of negative emotions and creates the biggest fear, allowing self-limiting beliefs to set in.

Lesson 1: The pillar that held us together

My father was my own pillar of strength, and that of our family. We were rock-solid and happy together. I was bold and fearless, a creative adolescent full of imagination. Nothing seemed impossible to me. I could take on the world, and this was what I did from nine years old all the way up to thirteen. I was completely in a world of my own. I even went to a multiracial school on the basis that my father thought education was paramount. He believed it was more important for me to get into other schools, gain a mixed-culture exposure because we were at the height of apartheid, and be ready when change came. He believed that change was inevitable, and that democracy was looming.

As things started breaking down, the political front was changing and the landscape slowly transforming; we had the option of going to a multiracial school, and I was one of the few children to go to one. Most kids didn't take this up due to fear, and the language barrier was also a huge deterrent. But I was this fearless thirteen-year-old. I went to this new school, new culture, new environment, but was comfortable with the transition. I made great friends and fitted in with excitement. This ability to take in change would later serve me well in life.

Lesson 2: Pain turned inwards

Until one early April day. I was in Grade 8, and my teacher suddenly came up to me and softly said, 'Victoria, you need to take your bag and come with me'. It was about ten o'clock in the morning. I wondered what had happened and had a deep sense of apprehension. I went with her to the office, and as I walked in, I saw my brother Sydney, the boxer, sitting there, talking to the Principal and waiting for me. He got up when he saw me, making formal greetings as we left. We got into the car, and there was no explanation, really. After a while, he just said, 'Dad is not well. So, you've got to get home'. I had left my father fine that morning. He was feeling a little bit off, but he was fine.

I could see as I walked through the gates that something was very wrong. There were people wailing. There were those with sad faces, and there were men standing with heads bowed. My father's friends, who used to sit on the porch, stood by the cars and were looking down. I knew something was terribly wrong. I didn't know what it would be, had no idea what was happening in our home. When I walked in, I noticed that the furniture was rearranged, and I felt a gush of coldness wash over my stomach. I was screaming inside, but my throat was dry. I couldn't do anything but enter mutely. There were elderly ladies sitting that I'd never seen in our home before.

I quickly ran straight into my father's bedroom, and as I opened the door, I could see that he was sleeping on the bed, but his whole body was covered all the way to his head. As I walked into the room, maybe two feet inside towards him, an auntie came, stopped me, and pulled me back, saying, 'No, no, no, you can't go in there'.

'Why?' I asked.

'He passed away.' And with that, she pulled me out and closed the bedroom door.

From that moment onwards, I felt like I was in a whirlwind. I became an invisible person because nobody saw me. Every adult in that room never explained anything to me or talked to me for that entire week. They didn't tell me why my dad passed away. I'd left my dad in good health when I went to school. And then, when I came home, he was gone, and no-one had told me what had happened to him. My mother was consumed with grief, and was being consoled by other people. I couldn't get to her. She couldn't get to me.

I had all these almost-strangers holding me and telling me it was going to be okay, but I didn't understand what was happening to start with. Why was my dad dead? It hit me hard. He was dead. He was never coming back. He was gone forever, and it seemed like a bad dream.

The reality of it hit me when one of dad's best friends, Tony Naidoo, started sobbing. He was an Indian guy, a boxing commentator who introduced boxers in a tournament. He had this wonderful, awesome voice that captivated thousands of people. Tony became my father's best friend through sports, and I'd often gone to go play in his house with his children. He used to come and sit with my father all the time. The penny dropped for me when this man, this huge, personality-filled, handsome, and well-dressed guy, walked towards our home. As he was walking towards the front porch, he was sobbing.

I looked at him and thought, 'Oh, that's how I'm feeling right now'. But I felt like I wasn't allowed to cry because I was told immediately when I walked in, 'It's okay, don't cry'. I'd held in my tears, but here was this man pouring and gushing his heart out. I wanted to be like him, but I couldn't. Somehow, that intensity of holding my tears in became my unresolved grief, my point of darkness.

Lesson 3: Cultural dynamics

In the Nguni culture, the mourning and bereavement period starts with the whole house being rearranged. The furniture's pushed aside, there's a wide-open space, and more chairs are added to the house. There were no tables, no cabinets, no television, nothing. Then, they would have memorial services every night. From morning to evening, the house was full of people coming in and out to pay respects to my father. Even our relatives from out of town came in to stay with us. Sleeping arrangements became something I didn't understand, even up to this day. We were sleeping on the floors, under the tables, on mattresses, on the chairs. Everywhere you could find a place with a little bit of a blanket, you slept. The whole week became a complete blur to me.

I didn't know what was happening. I couldn't comprehend anything, but the only thing I knew for sure at that time was that nobody expressed anything to me. Nobody spoke to me; no-one helped me understand what was happening. I became an invisible entity in the hustle and bustle of the household. In hindsight, I think that was a fundamental shift for me. I went into an emotional shell as a way of coping with the trauma of losing a loved one. This affected and reshaped my outlook on life as a carefree and spirited eleven-year-old.

Prior to this, I was this adolescent teenager who could take on the world—and suddenly, I started to question that. I felt I'd lost my seat at the table where I was seen. My father had made me feel important and relevant. My ideas had mattered to him. He'd poured out his thoughts and wanted to know how I felt and what I thought. This pillar of my strength had gone so suddenly, and my mind couldn't take this big change. It also felt like only adults were allowed to grieve and mourn openly. I kept my feelings bottled inside. Emotional support was crucial at that point, and to this day, I don't understand why children weren't given the freedom to grieve.

Lesson 4: Traumatic moments

In our culture, the whole bereavement process gives the family ample opportunity for full expression of grief. This allows mourners to move on with a normal life after the burial of a loved one. This is therapeutic to the family, who know they're not alone.

There would be a vigil with a lot of consoling and singing to uplift people in the home so that the mood wasn't so sombre. In hindsight, as an adult, I understood the reason behind the rituals and traditions; they were to support the bereaved family. That was meant to be therapeutic. It allowed mourners to cry and grieve the loss of a loved one. However, in our home in the week of bereavement and leading to the funeral, the community took over the house to assist with day-to-day activities. The constant flow of people and singing and prayer helped lift the mood, and the focus was to normalise the household after the funeral. The community wanted to ensure that the family could cope with the loss.

That part I understood as the culture's attempt to support a bereaved family. But my takeaway as a young child, at an impressionable age, was this: *Children were not to be seen or allowed to express their feelings of loss. This would have a negative impact on the emotional and mental wellbeing of the child or young adult.* This was the case for me for a long time, especially as a young adult. The fact was that nobody took the time to make me understand that I, too, could grieve the loss of my father. I had no self-regulating mechanism to support me. And I don't think anybody took that into account as they were going about the week, supporting us, and preparing for the funeral.

Children mostly remained unseen and uninvolved.

I don't know about my siblings, but they seemed to be fine. Tears didn't flow from them during that week, yet I think they were also going through their own grief. I found my older brother at the back of the house, shedding tears, and trying to hide it from me. Nobody had said to any of us, 'You're allowed to cry. It's okay to cry'.

I saw people, even my father's best friends, not displaying any emotions, except for Tony Naidoo. All the other men were keeping it in. The women were praying and singing, forming a constant circle around my mother. Her family members were there, aunts, uncles, and grandparents, but they were there for everyone else, not me. I was at the centre of my father's world every day. This newness of not being able to run to him, talk to him, or ask him questions tore me apart emotionally. My siblings, too, were never taken into confidence. They were never told what the process was, what needed to happen, or what had happened to our father. Sydney, the boxer-son, never stepped into the ring after the passing of my dad. I guess it hit him just as hard as well.

After the funeral, I got to find out what really happened to my father. The funeral was a massive event. At one point, I looked out through the bedroom window and saw the sheer number of people filling our street. Everybody had come to pay their respects to my father, and that's how I understood how big a man he was in the community. There were lots of priests, bishops, and senior pastors, all for a person who never went to church. Many from the sports and business sector also came to pay their tributes.

That day, seeing and hearing people talk about my dad and the fact that he was gone forever didn't bring closure, but a shock to my reality. I think I passed out at some point during the speeches. I was woken up later when everybody was getting up to leave for the cemetery. I'd missed most of the programme. Everything was kind of a blur. My emotions and behaviour were driven by the self-limiting belief of 'not being seen' and the negative processing of my loss. That's how the rug was really pulled out from under my feet.

Lesson 5: The grief that needed grieving

I went from a jolly, enthusiastic adolescent to feeling sad, lonely, hurt, and isolated. The grieving process is different for each person dealing with loss. Elisabeth Kubler-Ross documented five stages of grief that can help one overcome this tough period:

Denial, Anger, Bargaining, Depression, Acceptance. These can take anything from one to two years to process.

Parenting a child that had experienced loss or trauma as I did required a compassionate conversation that allowed the child's feelings to be ventilated. This would help process the different stages of grief and reach acceptance in a healthy way. This is a much-preferred option over the 'no conversation' approach that eventually leads to emotional withdrawal and isolation.

Parenting and caregiving has to be more than just provision of food and shelter, or driving kids to school and loving them. The love must be demonstrated in acts that resonate with children, touching all facets of their growing up and experiences they encounter. I know many families have experienced some kind of loss—whether from illness, the recent COVID-19 pandemic, death, or even divorce.

The latter is more prevalent in most societies, and for some unknown reason, children aren't trusted to understand when parents decide to divorce. Conversations are left until too late, when children show signs of withdrawal or are acting out. Parents focus on their own problems of not getting along, and one parent is left with the task of breaking the news and dealing with the fallout from this mess. Children are mostly not taken into confidence of why the adults have come to certain life-changing decisions. Adults need to step up, consider the impact on children, assure the children that it isn't their fault, and reassure them of their love and support.

These kinds of experiences traumatise children, who take the grief and pain upon themselves. At times, this isn't obvious to adults, because they're too engrossed in their own problems or pain. Unfortunately, this easily feels like neglect to children.

Becoming a quieter and more obedient child doesn't necessarily mean nothing's happening emotionally with them.

One of the symptoms of trauma or grief is the child's feeling that they did something wrong. They keep in all their feelings, which negatively alters their behaviour due to the unprocessed grief or trauma.

From my experience, I believe effective communication is very critical during this time. I know I needed a lot in my situation. It doesn't mean that if my parent or any of the relatives had sat me down and talked to me, I would've overcome whatever pain I was feeling at the time. I think grieving needs time and a process to resolve. *This could be from physiological symptoms, like insomnia, nightmares, and anxiety attacks because of the sudden awareness that this person isn't coming back.* They'll learn to cope and self-regulate through outside support.

There must be a compassionate approach taken to the child, teenager, or young adult, of explaining what happened, and acknowledging that having these big feelings are okay. Talking about my father, I later discovered he had renal failure, but I never saw him sick.

So, where did the renal failure come from, and why did it result in sudden death? Questions like this put so much pressure on the child, because they don't understand what's happening and start to imagine negative scenarios. Even though knowledge of my father's illness couldn't have been helped, it didn't stop me from wanting answers, resolving the hurt leading to irrational thoughts and behaviour.

How it evolved for me was that because of the loss of communication and not being seen, which is something I valued in my own state of mind. I drifted to thoughts of not being important, not being enough. I wondered how my life was going to be without my father. There was a deep sense of emptiness. I needed compassion. I needed some comforting, someone to understand what I was going through. I needed someone to hold my hand and be there for me.

My takeaway is that when someone's experiencing loss or grief without receiving emotional support, there's a likelihood they may seek external support or cling to something that will give them a sense of support. Or worse, they may drift away into self-isolation and depression, eventually impacting their quality of life.

Lesson 6: A call to caregivers

When caregivers and families don't support children during these difficult times—young adults especially—*they'll go out and find something or someone to comfort them to fill that void*. It might not be a good support mechanism, as I found out in hindsight.

If you're now a parent or caregiver, this is the one responsibility you can't afford to outsource simply because you have the child's best interests at heart. Someone else might not do what's good for the child. Instead, they might do what's good for themselves, or something against the values and principles you've taught the child. So, there's a lot of space where things can go emotionally wrong for the child and young adult. When children go to schools in this state of non-support, and they're feeling vulnerable, they're not strong, their self-esteem is low, and they're not themselves. Other children pick up on this negative energy. Children then start getting bullied, which alters their behaviour and school performance. Some young adults may even get into addictive substances. They can't defend themselves or consciously choose the right things in this state of low self-esteem. Without the correct intervention, it all starts spiralling downwards from that moment.

Lesson 7: The wrong support

As for me, I got attached to someone. We'll call him Themba (not his real name). Themba knew my father from the boxing gym. He was a youngster as well, a few years older than me. A few years later, after my dad had passed on, Themba came to our house looking for my sister, Maureen. He saw me coming from school and we started talking. I'd become a loner, keeping to myself after the loss of my dad. I mostly stayed at home, and didn't go out much. Books and studying were my solace, the place to hide my unresolved emotions.

Prior to this, our home was busy, loud, and fun. I recall a crazy ritual at home every other Saturday when my dad was still alive. On those days, the family would have spring-cleaning weekends. I could never understand it, because I thought the house was already clean. But rugs, carpets, and beds would be taken out and linen would be washed, and the house would be turned upside-down before it was put back to its original state again.

During this five-hour-plus crazy cleaning spree, I'd be sitting on the roof reading a book, running away from all the noise, hustle and bustle. I was young at the time, just getting out of everyone's way. And if I wasn't reading, I'd be hanging out with my dad, which was where I spent a lot of my time. Dad chose that time to visit his business mates and peers for sports engagement and meetings; anything outside the house, really. I think Dad was just running away from all the madness of cleaning going on. It would be about two o'clock that everything started to come back into place and normalise. And then later, if I was home, the aroma of lunch would indicate it was time to come down from the roof.

We went from moments of peaceful stability in our home to this void that I had within me. So, when Themba, the boxer who was familiar to me, approached me, which no other adult had done at that time, I felt seen, which was a different emotion.

I was a senior in high school at the time, a confusing period for any teenager. And in a multi-racial school too, which my father had said I should go to.

When we first talked, Themba listened, seeming interested in what I had to say. We had sports in common, which got us talking. He gave me compliments on my knowledge of boxing and sports in general. We got closer.

I'd longed for this kind of attention, and wasn't streetwise to boys at the time. I was excited that he was into boxing and that he'd progressed so well in the five years since my dad passed away. I was also intrigued by his discipline in training, which is something I'd seen in my father and brother. We'd talk about boxing matters all day when he visited me at home. I liked his persistence in pursuing me. We got close as friends at first, then it kind of spiralled from there, all the way from infatuation to a relationship.

I went from a place where I thought I was finally seen and into a relationship that heaped hot coals on my already vulnerable state of mind, dragging me deeper into darkness.

Practical tips for everyday life

- Grieving has its own time and process. Approach with compassion.
- Communication is key. There's a lot of space where things can go emotionally wrong for the child and young adult.
- Guide with patience and understanding. When grieving children go to school feeling vulnerable, they're not strong, their self-esteem is low, and they're not themselves. Other children pick up this energy and may not be kind.

6

INTERPERSONAL RELATIONSHIPS

Seasons of Feelings

*'You might have to fight a battle
more than once to win it.'*

—Margaret Thatcher

Have you ever been in a relationship, be it friendship, romantic, or collegial, and noticed 'red flags' popping up in the other person's behaviour? Did your intuition or inner voice whisper warnings to disengage? Did you hush these warnings or turn a blind eye? And did the 'red flags' become a field of fire?

Unknowingly, I gave up my freedom of choice when I chose to be ruled by fear. I drifted into a relationship which ended in a teenage pregnancy at age eighteen. I do hold myself responsible for what came next in my life, as I chose this relationship for the right and the wrong reasons. I ignored all the 'red flags' in pursuit of closing my emotional void. I became pregnant.

Lesson 1: What is your void? Are you relying on the relationship to close it, or complete you?

My drifting blindly or unconsciously into an unhealthy relationship was partly a coping mechanism for internalised grief. I'd suppressed my emotions, and the deflected pain led to new maladaptive behaviours. The relationship distracted me from my grieving, and I felt a different attention. It felt like a soothing balm, to be seen and acknowledged in this relationship.

However, this didn't stop that emotional pain. Instead, the pregnancy led to the condemnation and guilt I felt afterwards, which were even worse than the suppressed grief and pain. So, I became entangled in a different situation and a much darker emotional place. I had to live with a bad situation and emotional numbness.

I guess one must understand the power of suggestion when one's vulnerable. When pain isn't supported or addressed, and one doesn't get emotional support, it can be so impactful that it can change the course of one's life for the worse.

I was overwhelmed by the fact that I was a teenager about to complete high school, while being pregnant. I had to bear the immense judgement on me, and I felt condemned. I felt I'd brought my family shame and struggled to accept how I'd gotten myself into this mess.

My mom was still dealing with grief at this point. She was still trying to make sense of being the head of the family, and I felt that I'd let her down. But she also felt that she'd let my father down. So, I was in a very precarious situation as a teenager, and all rational thoughts had flown out of the door. I soon learned of the consequences of an unaligned relationship resulting from thoughtlessness.

During this period, both of us (i.e. Themba and I), being young as we were, were thrown into a relationship without thought. With undefined dreams, the process disturbed and distracted us. We had a change of perspective and heart. What was once fun now seemed like a burden and a chore, and I had to become an adult very quickly.

That's the danger of being a vulnerable teenager who's struggling with emotions that are suppressed—your behaviour shows your pain. Have you ever felt like your life was drifting aimlessly without any clear direction?

As a young adult, the danger of having all these unresolved emotions takes away your focus from your own desires and plans.

One tends to focus so much on the fear of the unknown, as well as the guilt and condemnation that comes with it. I think society can be too harsh as well sometimes. They put pressure on you when you're too vulnerable to make any decision, at a time when there's no emotional support to help you out. I think the worst thing is to be pressured into other people's plans when you, yourself, haven't thought about who you are and what you want. You end up kind of following suit, whether to please a family or partner or for cultural and social compliance.

We tend to tick the social boxes for appearance's sake and keep pressure at bay, avoiding looking at our weaknesses. And that lowers one's self-esteem even further, as it did mine. My own internal beliefs were compromised.

I'd temporarily lost the ability to listen to my own intuition and act on it like I used to.

Suddenly, I was second-guessing myself. I was full of self-doubt, and because I was in this emotional limbo mode, others felt like they could play a leadership role in my life. I felt like I was in a total bubble of just following others without thought of what I wanted out of my own life. I couldn't seem to make sense of my own desires.

At some point, I felt like I was living someone else's life. I had an out-of-body experience from a distance once. I was looking at my life and thinking, 'Whose life is that, and who is that girl? How did I end up here?'. I'd changed so much that I couldn't even recognise myself. But the interesting part, which I think happens to most people, is that we carry on living, and days roll into years.

Lesson 2: The internal burden that no-one sees

Inside, we're suffering, but on the outside, we're living. We mask our real and authentic selves. People don't see the emotional scars we carry internally. We perpetuate the dysfunction to appear okay.

To me, what was once a very familiar place, that of courage and confidence, became unfamiliar. And disconnecting from my inner voice became familiar. I kind of drifted along with it. To avoid the taboo situation I found myself in, I became a social pleaser. I was ticking the social expectation box and got married.

Prince Charming alert: Well, there was no Prince Charming in my life, nothing like what I had read in many Mills and Boon novels of being swept off your feet, being romanced, and having a glorious wedding. In our culture, the marriage procedure involves 'lobola', a kind of dowry to the girl's family, ideally given before any pregnancy. So, we skipped this big step, to my mother's dismay and adding salt to the wounds of shame. Why, you might ask? At the time, I was emotionally unavailable and didn't challenge any suggestions he made. I accepted everything naively or was nonchalant about it. It started with the rings. Themba and I walked past a jewellery store when he, out of the blue, said, 'Do you want a ring? We should get married'.

Before I could think or respond, we were walking into the store. I finally thought, 'Why not?'. And I said, 'Yeah sure'. I loved jewellery like most women. Also, it invoked sweet old memories of being in a jewellery store; I felt giddy. The proposal came as he was about to travel abroad on a sports tour for three months. We got to his mom's house to show her the rings, to which she responded very unemotionally, saying 'Ah, nice' and walking away.

Instinctively, I knew that wasn't a happy response, but what was I to do? We'd been dating for a few years, and I thought the ring might make things good; no more shame for all concerned. *This was a red flag that popped up, one of many, and I looked the other way.* Ever been in that situation yourself?

Anyway, we got married soon after his return from overseas. It wasn't what I particularly desired, but something I did for the social pressure. Not 'being yourself' shows up in many ways. In short, there were no wedding plans, no bridesmaids or groomsmen, no family from both sides. That is how emotionally absent I was with the process that unfolded.

Lesson 3: People-pleasing makes everybody happy except you

The day before the wedding, I was informed that his manager got him a 'marriage license' and the appointment was the following day. I was surprised and asked, 'We are getting married tomorrow?'. In shock and confusion, I said, 'But I don't have anything to wear'.

That wasn't the correct question to ask, but vain me (*an emoji with hand over face*) was a naïve and foolish twenty-one-year-old.

He responded, 'I took care of it and got you a dress!'. When you're in a daze, it feels good when someone else is taking the lead, as you don't want to THINK. So, I was married on a Thursday, at 9 am at the Magistrates' Court. Well, I can't tell you whether I answered *I can*, *I will*, or *I shall* in response to the vows, as it was a quick and a blurry moment. Oh, on the wedding dress, it was a lovely silk cocktail dress with taffeta sleeves. *A stunner that fitted my petite body like a glove. Well, kudos to whoever got me the dress, as I never got to know.* In a way, I was swept off my proverbial feet in this wedding. Once I realised we were going to spend time at his mom's home, I negotiated to get a place of our own. The latter was a deal-breaker; I managed that much. I stayed there three months as *makoti* (newly married woman) at his home. I soon learned what in-law demeanour meant.

Five days after moving into our new home, I told my sister-in-law (and friend still today), Yayi, who visited, 'I don't think I should have married this guy'. She looked at me blankly and asked, 'What are you saying?!'. I just looked at her and held her gaze as it dawned on me that I'd expressed my thoughts out aloud. I was embarrassed.

Intuitively, I realised two things: One, I shouldn't have married the guy, and the other, I didn't do it because I wanted to, but to tick the social box. I followed the expectation that you get married to take away the guilt, condemnation, and shame that you brought upon the family. Sadly, that didn't happen.

Fear is a very powerful emotion, and it can come from pain, trauma, and external pressure that, if you can't deal with it or get help to deal with it, will automatically paralyse you and hold you hostage. Then, your life is never the same if you don't do anything about it.

Lesson 4: We get into relationships for different reasons. What's yours?

There's an old saying that relationships are sometimes temporary, for a season or for a lifetime. *The latter works when individuals in it are emotionally stable, not seeking to be 'completed' or validated by the relationship. Also, it happens when one is allowed to grow within the relationship in pursuing one's own dreams plus joint goals.*

The question, though, is what value can one offer in a relationship if they *don't* believe in their own worth, who they are, and what they want? When we go into relationships for the wrong reasons, and don't think about the type of relationships we want, we set ourselves up for failure.

I never thought much about the type of relationship I wanted. I was responding to the pressure of the situation I found myself in, also driven by the fact I was an ignorant teenager. I suppressed my own intuition and didn't allow myself to become my authentic self in the relationship I found myself in. The lack of effective communication was evident.

As young people tell me, getting into interpersonal relationships is hard. This is worsened by social media and the pressure it brings. Both parties might start with different ends in mind. Think about what your end goal is and how a relationship connects with this. Think about the timing and your own readiness. It must not be a tick off a checklist like it was for me, or validation-seeking, or for financial gain and peer pressure.

I get told by young ladies that it's hard to find good partners that stay. I always respond with a question. Do you know what you want, or do you just want to be in a relationship? I get responses that reflect the young, uncertain person I once was, of not knowing who you are and where you're heading with your life. If you have no clarity about who you are, what you want out of life, then 'it's hard'.

If you determine that your relationship must align with your set plans, what the relationship should look like, what value you bring and expect back, and what your boundaries are as informed by your values, then you'll attract the right interpersonal relationship. If not, then you'll drift into a behaviour that has nothing to do with who you are and your desires, as I found out in my first relationship.

The fundamental lesson for me was to be clear about knowing myself, what I wanted out of life, and the connection and chemistry that I seek in a relationship. If you are emotionally vulnerable and can't decide what you want out of your life, you'll be trapped. I was, and it wasn't cool not living my best life.

I think things are a bit different now in 2024 than when I was younger. Teenagers and young adults are now exposed to far more information, as it's a global village. They could be talking to anyone at any given point in time. So, I think it becomes imperative that parents, families, and societies are aware of where their child is emotionally and what their levels of emotional stability and needs are.

I recently went to my local hair salon, and a young lady was assisting my hairstylist. She was new, and we struck up a casual conversation that went deep very quickly. Just by asking if she was taking a gap year, she answered, 'I am not sure what I want to do'.

I asked further, 'Any interest in your life, like hair or music or reading?'.

She responded, 'I haven't thought much about it … what I want'.

Aghast, I pressed on, 'Have you talked it out with your parents or someone close?'.

Her response was, 'Oh, they won't listen to me. It's like I am not there, even though I am struggling and need emotional support from them. By the way, adulting sucks'.

This was hard to hear but I understood her, as I'd had a similar experience at her age. I told her to call me so we could chat more privately and give her guidance.

When parents or families know that something's happened that might have caused pain, trauma, or grief to a person or member of the family, efforts must be made to support that person. The sooner the intervention starts, the better. It's important that the person receives support for the pain from the trauma or hurt that they're going through and not be left to their own devices, as negative emotions can easily consume one and stay stuck for years to come.

The thoughts from those negative energies and emotions quickly change one's life, and people find it hard to get out of this mode. Soon, one loses hope and their path. That's why one must be assisted at some point with intervention by family or professionals.

With today's kids—the Millennials and Gen Zs—who have access to so much information, the voids in their lives can be closed by anyone or anything. So, parents, caregivers, family and relatives must closely watch what's happening emotionally to the person. I'm grateful that, in my case, my mother came to my rescue and was the crucial lifeline that I held on to in my emotional storm.

Practical tips for everyday life

- When pain isn't supported or addressed, and when one's not receiving emotional support, this can be so impactful that it can change the course of one's life for the worse.
- If you haven't clearly defined who you are, what you want out of life, how the relationship aligns with your plans, and what the relationship should look like, you'll drift into a behaviour that has nothing to do with who you are.

- It's best to know what you want out of a relationship and have clarity for yourself first. Otherwise, if you're emotionally vulnerable and can't decide what you want out of your life, you'll be trapped.

Endnotes

www.sadag.org
www.mind.betterme.world.com

7

A CRUCIAL LIFELINE

Curious Mindset

*'Love expressed between two women is particular
and powerful because we have to love in order to live;
love has been our survival.'*

—Audre Lorde

During the craziness in my life, at the depth of my own negative emotions and while continuing to spiral downwards, I was rescued from my deep, dark, emotional place by the very person I felt had mostly let down: my mom. I'd thought there was no one for me. I was drowning in despair, but a crucial lifeline was given to me, and hope came in the form of my own mother.

My mother's kindness and compassionate approach disarmed me from all anxiety and pent-up emotion when we sat down together. We had one of the first honest and heartfelt conversations I could recall since the passing of my father.

I apologised for it all. She apologised. We wept and hugged, and she promised that she'd be there for me. She said that she'd help me take care of the baby, admonishing me that we mustn't let down my father, who had expectations for me to finish school and university.

Lesson 1: Support builds strength

We talked about Dad and how we missed him. I was relieved and got excited that my dreams were reignited. I felt like I had a second chance, and she demanded that I finish school and university. This was the positive effect of forgiveness; it builds inner strength and liberates you. All these events happened when I was almost giving up and had decided to settle for where I was at. But when I had this ray of hope that had just sprung from her forgiveness, I took a second breath. I was able to summon a glimmer of hope from within.

For gold to be made, it must go through the hottest heat and pressure. And the metal comes out sparkling on the other side.

As bad as what had happened to me was up to this point, I'm grateful for these tough life experiences in retrospect. I don't wish trauma on anyone, but we can't escape life's challenges; it's how we get through them that makes us stronger. In my case, I was a young mother and needed to be responsible, so trauma made me a better and stronger person.

When you face intense pressure, it can either break you or help you come out stronger, brighter, and more resolved.

That was the option I took: to come out stronger and more resolved to win, to claim my life back. My mother's love and support opened my heart to try again. I recall memories of my Dad and how he'd groomed winning boxers. At the time, I'd been too young to fully understand and appreciate the mental strength training he was building into the minds of the boxers. The boxers didn't always train physically. Sometimes, Dad had them do the movement anyway, repeating affirmations as they did, working on their mental focus.

My father would drill certain positive affirmations into them, saying, 'You're the champion', amidst many other positive affirmations. The boxer may be punching a bag or doing shadow boxing, but he'd also be running these affirmations through his head. And I'd ask Dad later, 'Why are they doing that? And why is there no other person in the gym?'.

He'd say, 'I don't need anyone in the gym during this time, because Sydney needs to focus on his mental strength'.

Lesson 2: The mindset training

I recall that my brother had once lost a fight to the legendary Makhathini and that my father hadn't taken it as badly as I thought he would. With each victorious fight, everybody celebrated. And after a loss, they'd be down, but my father was never down. He'd be the first one to stand up and say with confidence, 'Champ, we misjudged this boxer and we should do certain things differently next time'. He told my brother, 'We'll be better prepared next time. And I'm telling you; you won't even go the full distance with this guy. He won't know what hit him because he thinks he's got you now, but we're going to do something better and different to surprise him next time'.

They put in the work, reviewing tapes of previous fights, analysing them, and coming up with a plan to do it differently. This involved thousands of hours in preparation for a thirty-six-minute match.

That's where I think mental strength came in. My brother never lost to the legendary Makhathini again in their two rematches thereafter. In hindsight, I understood that Dad was preparing me for situations that I wasn't aware of. He was teaching that mental strength is necessary to face hardships. Denzel Washington has a famous saying: *You fall seven times, and you get up eight times.* When we drove together, Dad used to remind me about these facts. He would be so quiet for long moments, and I'd say, 'Dad, why are you so quiet? You don't want to switch on the radio or something?'.

He'd say, 'No, I'm thinking'. So, from him, I also learned the importance of deep thinking and grew to love those silent moments. I learned to sit in silence too, doing my own thinking.

He had certain things that he loved to do. One was to quietly watch the opening ceremonies of the Parliament of the apartheid government, and he'd ask me to sit with him and watch. This wasn't a popular event in those days, as this broadcast was done in the Afrikaans language. Now, the State of the Nation Address (*Sona*) is well-watched under the democratic dispensation, but not back then. Dad would share insights about the Parliament because he wanted me to be aware of the impact that our leaders' decisions would have on us as a people. He encouraged me to be aware of my environment and its influence. Because he was involved in many areas like sports and business, he also had access to crucial information that could impact us. From Dad, I learned that mental strength was imperative for victory and progress in various areas. He prioritised mental strength. *In hindsight, it was always a matter of mind over matter.*

Lesson 3: Learn to never waste second chances

This opportunity, this second chance that came from my mother's compassion, ignited something within me. I became positive for the first time in a long while. The positivity and confidence slowly started creeping back. And then, because of my positive state of mind, the eleven-year-old self came into my mind and questioned me.

When you become aware of where you are and where you've been, and you start questioning what happened to you and why you're here, the awareness of where you want to be suddenly faces you. You realise that you're not where you're supposed to be. And this massive gap shows up, indicating you've moved far away from your desires and vision for your life. But the reality says 'You are here', and you must live in the moment you're in.

To accept the things that have happened to you is a start. I accepted that I was a young mother. I'd finished school and had to go to university. So, that muscle and mental memory that was buried underneath started re-germinating and showing signs of life. As a young mom struggling to pay the fees for the university, I opened a salon; making hair became my hustle in a bid for me to be able to afford things as a young mom.

However, I couldn't stop there. I realised it wasn't a sustainable business, nor the endgame for me. It was just there to fill a short-term need.

Lesson 4: Hard knocks are the school of life

When you open yourself to the positive energy of love and optimism, the universe does conspire to support you. In my case, shortly after the salon stint, there was an offer to be trained as a machinist for high school graduate. I applied for this initiative that prepared students to get into the job market. I knew at the time that I couldn't afford university, but this was a different kind of learning. I was recruited for this programme, and they paid a stipend. As a young mom, I needed this.

This role was not very popular, as it entailed working in a factory and sewing clothes. I wasn't bothered by what was being said, as I needed to get busy and out of the township. My needlework training came in handy. In no time, I was producing quality work and even assisting others. The supervisors picked up on this and called me in for a chat. They asked what was happening, and I told them I was just helping others struggling with tension to improve quality. They asked if I'd done my quota and passed quality checks, to which I responded in the affirmative.

From then on, I got a different role—that of a supervisor trainer. The leadership part in me began to emerge in subtle ways. I knew everything happened for a reason; nothing is coincidental, as we tend to think. I got an opportunity to sharpen my dreams. These were seeds starting to germinate, and gave me the reinforcement that I was going in the right direction. The positivity kept pouring in, and with that, I continued to push and challenge myself.

Lesson 5: Be bold in your pursuit of opportunities

After the intern programme came to an end, my sister-in-law, Edith, a nephrology nurse (and Sydney's wife), brought me some application forms; her hospital was recruiting nurses. The first thing I asked was, 'Oh, how much do they pay?'. That was the indicator of my attitude and outlook on life at the time, because I was pressed into survival mode. When I heard about the nursing opportunity, which was in patient care, I realised I could study and get paid. Plus, learning this field aligned with my desires to study further and specialise. Edith explained how it worked. Grateful to her, I knew that the love and support was always there, but I had never looked up to it before.

This new gig appealed to my self-development goals, so there was no hesitation in enrolling and studying at Groote Schuur Hospital in Cape Town. I had had good results in my high school exams, and ended up graduating top of my class. You know what? I loved it; the service to others was what surprised me the most about myself. It warmed my heart to know that I was contributing goodness.

Lesson 6: Do things that lift your confidence

Everything works together for our good. In the moment, you might not realise that you're impacting your future by the decisions that you're making today. But you are!

I quickly realised that nursing isn't for the faint-hearted. It's hard work which requires dedication. I loved the work of patient care, and studying something new made me feel valuable. Also, I could take care of my family during this phase, which was my reality and need. And the most important factor that I think I connected with nursing is my love for people and being of service.

Nursing, from a theoretical point of view, was pretty much easy, interesting, and fun. It appealed to my love of books, studying, adventure, and learning new things. I decided that I'd go to university once I graduated from the nursing programme. I became interested in counselling psychology, so I knew I'd study psychology at university. I was looking ahead to what would naturally follow due to my enthusiasm and positive mindset. It was those moments that enabled me to connect the dots of my purpose, passion, and North Star.

Towards the end of my nursing career and training, I'd assist doctors with their patients as a multi-lingual nurse. I became a popular choice for doctors to bring along on their rounds. I ended up having a different level of exposure, working in cross-functional and management teams at the hospital.

Lesson 7: Each experience is a journey of discovering your strengths

The nursing role gave me a different perspective on my strength in communication. Once again, my confidence was slowly being built up because I felt valued and seen. I was rewarded for being known throughout the hospital for my positive and cheerful disposition. People knew I was a capable and reliable nurse, and this made me feel good about myself, as I was doing something of value. The momentum of being busy with something else charged up my optimism. I became a stronger person because my outlook in life was now reassured. I had a level of certainty that I didn't have before. I knew that things would work out.

I had another responsibility besides work and study: I had to settle into the role of being a young wife. I used the muscle and mental memory that came back to me to negotiate my way forward in the situation I found myself in. Fortunately, I was able to negotiate to go to the university after the stint in nursing, even though I was a young wife. After I'd completed the course to receive a diploma, I struck a deal with my partner that carried me forward towards one of my other goals.

It's amazing how much energy you have when you're in a positive mindset. When your thoughts are directed to the things that you want, you have incredible energy. So, I focused more on solutions than on problems.

Lesson 8: Strength creates life purpose

Previously, I was in a place where all I could think about my life was being in the negative mode and being stuck. I thought of condemnation, I thought of fear, I thought of shame, and I thought I'd let down myself and my family. But because I had a child, and with my mother's support and compassion, I felt I'd been given a second chance. I got to a point of deciding that I could start taking on bigger responsibilities to close the gaps to my goals.

I became relentless in pursuing my dreams now that I'd shifted perspective and knew that I wasn't alone. I had the definite mindset that I was going to go to university. I was going to study psychology and become a psychologist. I had a purpose and a new drive in life. That rekindled my energy, and I developed an 'I can do this' attitude. I was a mother now. I was a nurse. I had a profession and a career, but I wanted more out of life. This hope just kept on pushing me and pushing me forward with a positive outlook. I was still married, I still had that life, and I had to carry on living there as well. But I just kept pushing forward to define my purpose and insisted on working on myself and my goals.

Lesson 9: The resilient mentor in my life

The most grateful part of facing those years was the role model that I found in my mom. I appreciate that her presence helped me bloom.

Born Enid Schultz, a mixed-race second-generation offspring of an African (Xhosa) father and a German mother, my mom was fondly known as *Mampondo*, loosely translated as 'horns' (her father's clan name). She was the silent type and a soft-spoken beauty. She spoke with her face and expressions. My mother would tell me, 'Don't do that' with her eyes, and she'd smile to tell me, 'I love you'. My mother had to deal with her own grief and become a single parent and head of a home overnight. Prior to this, she was a housewife, since Dad was the provider and took care of her. But after he passed, I saw tremendous strength and courage in her, as she took over my father's businesses. My mom became an entrepreneur, but her generosity, kindness, and compassion never wavered.

We had a policy in my home that everybody was welcome, and my mother continued that legacy. She was a caregiver. She was a mother to everyone who met her. She was a woman who had the ability to adapt, and she never complained about her lot. She was a true inspiration in resilience. I admired her many facets. While my father was the pillar of strength, my mother was the pillar of resilience, one who continued with determination and compassion despite hardships.

By the time she passed, my mother and I were best friends, bless her soul. She was my confidant and cheerleader. And I'm grateful that she was a role model for me. I thank God for her life and wise counsel. Because of her, I can now do the same for my own children. With my mother's support and wisdom, I could finally breathe and feel able to pursue my desires. Thank you, Mom, for the unconditional love that grounded me to ask myself a tough question.

My parents, each in their own way, stepped up for me and became great role models. They left me with a legacy of kindness regarding how to be a role model in my own life for my own children, as well as to others.

Think of the people who populate your life. Think of their influence and how they support you. *Who are you, and what do you want out of this life?*

Practical tips for everyday life

- There's always a reason for everything in our lives. Everything works together for our good. In the moment, you might not see that the decisions that you're making today are really impacting your future. But you are.
- It's amazing how much energy you have when you are in a positive mindset, when your thoughts are directed to the things you want.
- When you gain the awareness of where you are and where you've been, you start questioning what happened to you and why you're here. Then, the awareness and the prompting of where you want to be suddenly faces you.
- Your dreams are the clues to the possibilities that exist in your life.

8

WHO YOU ARE

Pondering Your Identity

'Be yourself; everyone else is already taken.'

—OSCAR WILDE

I can't answer what I want unless I know who I am. Everything starts and ends with knowing the real, unique me. Everyone searches for a meaningful life at some point. It becomes worthwhile to pursue one's own answer to this fundamental question: *Who are you?* Can one *really* answer the question of what they want unless they know who they are?

Lesson 1: Recognising the mask

In my case, life was happening to me and coming at me in both my personal and business life. I was past the point of just drifting away, with no thoughts of 'Who are you?'. I was merely existing and had no control over my destiny. But the room to breathe and catch my breath, so to speak, gave me a moment to pause. The eleven-year-old Victoria came up in my mind and asked, 'Who are you? Why are you not in the plan for your dreams?'. That was the strong, young Victoria—a fearless, full-of-faith girl who could do anything she put her mind to. She was gone, albeit temporarily.

This question is true for all who want to find their own purpose and meaning in life. We must all start by answering this question. This is a simple yet complex question, as I came to find out.

Who are you? Have you given it any thought? Or are you like me, and never gave this any thought for a long time?

Are you in touch with who you are? And is there an alignment between who you are and who you're becoming?

What are your dreams and desires? Have you given these much thought?

Or is it okay to define ourselves based on the roles and functions of society? Do we define ourselves as mothers, teachers, corporates, sisters, entrepreneurs, and other identities?

Is who you are what you do? Or is who you are what others say about you?

Are these competencies of ours subsets of who we are? Do these roles inform our characters and shape us? *Yet, they don't answer,* ***Who am I?*** Or do they?

The grace I received gave me the pause that allowed me to step back away from social judgement, away from my own condemnation of my mistakes. The pause allowed me to consciously think about these questions: *Who am I and what do I want? What are my desires out of this life and for my loved ones?* It seemed I was a bystander looking into my life—no personal vision, no structure, no plans or goals. At the time, I was just floating aimlessly as a young wife.

In hindsight, I understand that I was just muddling along, living. Internally, I was in emotional turmoil, but on the outside, I looked okay. The emotional mask was on, obscuring me. That's why it's so important to look at this question with the significance it deserved.

Lesson 2: What do you really want from life?

I hear this a lot these days from young people: 'My life is hard; I want more'. Sometimes, they'd say more money, more career growth, more nice things. When I ask further to try and get to specifics by asking 'Who are you?', they pause and quickly say, 'Mmm … I don't know how to answer that because I've never thought about it'. I sometimes get a look like I'm asking a trick question. Because when I say, 'If you have more money, then what?', the answer is: 'I don't know'. They haven't answered who they are to inform what they want.

Who are you and what do you want out of your life? What's the purpose and meaning you seek in life? What's your life story?

For me, there was no harmony between my present situation and what I'd thought would be my life in my early years. There was a big discord. I'm grateful for the pause that allowed me a quiet time for self-reflection. This enabled me to evaluate myself at all these crucial moments that were gifted to me. I realised that my various vulnerable states had changed me unconsciously. I'd drifted and followed others and had become a people-pleaser. I couldn't stand up for myself or communicate my needs and wants. I silenced my own vision and values. I ended up living for everyone else, except me. That's why this question is such a fundamentally important one. We can't carry on life without asking these questions of ourselves: Who am I and what do I want out of this life? And what meaning do I attach to my experiences?

Thanks to the role model of my mom, as well as my colleagues, family, and friends who believed in me, hope came in various ways, even though I was struggling emotionally. This hope allowed me to understand certain aspects of my own behaviour. I got to understand why I'd suddenly become a person who was pleasing others, not following my intuition, and going after things I really wanted.

Lesson 3: Taking time to ponder

This pondering got me to a place of saying, 'I need to use my time to contribute to my own life story, rather than everyone else's life'. I had to stop this feeling that I was constantly on the treadmill of life and that there were constant demands on me for others' benefit rather than my own. I became mindful of this—and in that awareness, I had a choice to stop or do nothing. I had a choice to redefine the things I wanted. This took courage and being intentional. This took faith and certainty without being fixated on the 'how'.

I had to delve deep and look at my life and what I wanted for my children. Also, what did I want for myself? What kind of quality of life did I want? I had to be clear and specific about it. I had to figure out my identity; where was it really embedded?

I had to do a self-check without any judgements.

My self-talk shapes who I am. Be aware of who you say you are. Are you optimistic or cynical, ambitious or uninspired, a constant worrier or confident? These come from what you say to yourself.

Answering who you are prompts you to create a personal vision that will lead to your own defined success. Knowing your identity drives and compels you to act on the things you want for yourself. Identity does really matter; it allows you to 'see you' and appreciate who you are.

The beauty in this is that you can still answer this question at any point in your life, so it's never too late to start. In my case, as a curious person, I was committed to changing my life for the better, and needed to regroup mentally and emotionally. I had to start my self-check exercise and did a SWOT analysis from the toolsets gained from years of operational executive and coaching.

Lesson 4: Do a personal SWOT

Throughout my career, I've used lots of tools and tactics to solve business challenges, enabling continuous improvements, and adding value and growth. However, I never used these in my personal life for some obscure reason. Yet the motivation to improve my lot led me to think of applying the personal SWOT analysis, which is a strategic evaluation framework.

This enabled me to think and review my Strengths, Weaknesses, Opportunities and Threats. It was clear to me that there were gaps that signalled that I wasn't okay, and that I was off the mark when I answered each one relative to self, family, career, or business. It gave me a starting point to evaluate *my life account's balance sheet.* The SWOT gave me a view of my internal (*within my control*) and external (*outside my control*) influences and positive and negative attributes about myself.

PERSONAL SWOT ANALYSIS

The analysis revealed that my threat was having no personal vision, as well as no core vision of who I was and what I wanted.

Lesson 5: The manuals of life

I stumbled upon an interesting insight, and I'll give you a metaphorical example of it. I'm sure you must have bought a brand-new phone, computer, or something else that came packaged in a box. I found out that people who owned the same or similar brand unbox, unwrap, and just use it without checking the manuals.

I ask the question, 'Do you go through the manual?' Ninety per cent of the people say, 'No, I don't bother because I know how to switch it on and I figure it out without really looking at the manuals'.

My curious mind took that example and transposed it to ourselves to figure out our identity.

Here I have this package called *Me* and I'm trying to figure out my identity. If I don't have a manual, what else can I do? I probably do what other people say they do. They toss the manual away and just figure it out as they go, like the computer example.

My question was, and still is: What if this new version has a function or upgrade that you're not aware of and that you can only know about if you read the manual from the manufacturer? Perhaps there could be some smart dynamics you can apply? Or do you just use that device in a trial-and-error manner? Most of the time, people respond, 'It's trial and error. I only find out later that, oh, I can also do many other things. Otherwise, I just use the basic stuff that I already know'. They're not using their full potential because they're not aware of what's inside and the power of the computer. I know this is a simplistic view. But that's why Apple Inc holds tutorials daily for its phones, as users just don't check manuals to maximise the device's full potential. (Okay! I digress, being an Apple user!)

Most of us, I believe, go through life like that. We kind of assume our roles, get into them, drift along, and float along until we have what I always call a painful moment that shocks us into accepting the reality of our experiences. Then, you pause and observe. You question, 'Wait a minute. Where am I? Why is this happening to me?'. Most of us do this same thing. But this pause could serve as a good turning point for that purposeful life we're longing for.

To shift my perspective, I became curious. I asked myself, 'If I had to look for a "manual" for Victoria, what would that manual be like?'. People say, 'Well, go to your clan. You must have a tribe. You must have a family lineage. You must have a family root that will show you where you came from'. I suppose I can take that path, but I think the most important thing I've stumbled on is the oldest book in the world, the Bible. (Let's note that I was sceptical when it came to religion at that time in my life.)

Lesson 6: Finding the strength to let go of the pain

In the early part of my marriage, I constantly faced situations that triggered the 'fight or flight' reaction. I was in a toxic relationship that was abusive. I was suffering.

On a particular day, the threat to my life ramped up high. My ex-husband was driving, and he punched me in the face while in a fast-moving car on the motorway. It was too much to bear, and I opened the door and threw myself out of the speeding vehicle. I landed hard on the road. No, I wasn't being a stuntwoman—but on that day, logic left me, and the instinct of survival kicked in.

Fortunately for me, there were no speeding cars behind, except one that swerved out of the way to miss me by inches and stopped. I managed to get up and ran towards the car. I opened the door, jumped into the back seat, and said, 'Drive, please'. I crouched behind, and as the car sped off, I looked up from the backseat. The drivers were two young, coloured men with scary tattoos covering their face and arms.

They asked me, 'Who was that guy?'. I told them the truth about the abuse, and they asked where I wanted to be dropped off. I said at my mother's, which was the closest place I could go. They took me there, got out of the car, and walked with me. They talked to my mother and explained everything. I remember them asking my mother if they should wait for my ex 'to sort him out'.

My mom, not one for conflict, thanked them and sent them on their way. I was in pain, both internally and externally.

How that day ended was another source of hurt for me. My family, bless their hearts, had good intentions. They told me they'd talked to the abuser and calmed him down, that it seemed to be a misunderstanding, according to his explanation. He'd managed to charm everyone.

Oh, the things we endure for societal belonging, I was told to go home with him and that it would be okay. As I walked out of the house, something raw in my emotions surfaced for the first time, and I longed for my father. I missed him terribly. I thought I wouldn't be bullied this much if he was around.

I resigned myself that I was alone. I survived that ordeal, but I was resolute that I wanted out of this mess of a marriage. Thanks to what came next, I was able to let go of that toxic relationship.

Fast-forward to two weeks later. My mother asked me to accompany her to a funeral on the first of January. Her friend's grandson had tragically lost his life in an accident. I agreed as I wasn't in a very festive mood, given the internal turmoil I was going through at the time. Culturally, women don't go to the cemetery due to the nature of death. We were left behind at home. All the women started praying and consoling each other. I was used to this, which had been an uneventful thing for me in the past. This time, I didn't expect much either, until a young lady in her twenties stood up and talked about her loving father. She prayed and said she thanked God that she had a father in the heavenly places, that she wasn't alone, and that her father would never leave or forsake her. Then, she asked if we knew our father in heaven, and if we had a relationship with our divine maker? She further insisted that her divine father has promises stored for her to prosper even in this tough world we live in.

This intrigued me. It wasn't like I'd never heard this before, but there was a subtle nuance I picked up. I am not like a super-religious person, and only went to church occasionally. However, this resonated with me differently because I was in the process of mentally searching for an answer, and was longing for my father as well.

Lesson 7: Rediscovering my father's love

I was missing my dad and longing for him to help me out. This lady was talking about a father who created you. She challenged the audience, saying, 'We know him and all the promises in store for us, and the support through burdens like today's funeral'. I was intrigued by how coolly and confidently she spoke, not to mention the courage to address elders. This was unheard of, a young person speaking with such authority in a very sombre gathering. She got my full attention. There was a spark of hope in my heart, and in my mind, I thought, 'I can take a gamble and try this too; get more understanding of these promises'.

As she was saying, 'The Father knows the plans that He has for you, the plans not to hurt you, plans to give you a future and hope and a sound mind'. These things kind of blew me away, as if it were a sign, a message from my father. Because I was in an open-minded heart space, with recent traumatic experiences, it felt like I was hearing the words for the first time. And I guess that's how, for me, things started to come together. It began with the awareness and acknowledgement that I have a father. And that's how I encountered the Divine, the infinite love and intelligence. It was outside church walls or from a priest, as I would have expected. But the words came from a young woman who embodied love, faith, confidence and courage.

This thought alone got me excited that I was coming closer to figuring things out for my life. The void that I'd always felt that the young thirteen-year-old Victoria was seeking kind of came together in that moment. It became a revelation and a great insight for me, and I couldn't stop myself from becoming excited and curious with expectation.

The young lady challenged all of us to go and 'talk to your father today. Tell him your burden and ask for guidance. And then believe and wait in expectation by faith'.

I did just that. I got home and went, 'Ok, I'm giving this a shot'. The gambler in me realised the stakes were high; well, I had nothing to lose. I followed her instructions to a T.

I fell to my knees in the centre of my beautiful mansion, which had become a prison for me. And I talked to God and asked for help. I remember saying: *I cannot do this by myself anymore. I am tired.*

Two weeks before this insight, I had had a near-death experience. That is how it all unravelled for me. But after the encounter, I was overcome with calmness, as I felt release from something buried deep within. It was a cathartic moment. I loved the feeling of being unafraid that enveloped me.

I found the courage to file for divorce, and peace embraced me.

Following that day, I started to notice many coincidences that were messages. For example, while randomly TV channel–hopping, the channel would stop on a programme where someone would say: 'You are not alone' or 'You have a father in heaven'.

I had repeated vivid dreams of a dinosaur coming in the front door, only that I wasn't afraid of it. As it walked into the house, I walked backwards as it demolished the house with its tail, leaving behind a trail of bricks. It disappeared when I was at the door frame. I told adults about it, including my mom's friend, Aunt Winnie, who said, 'Ay, no! I don't like that dream at all. Why demolish the beautiful house?'. My silent thought was, 'I don't mind. I wish it could be real'.

I checked out my thoughts right there, and I knew I wanted out.

I continued to search for 'Who am I,' and the calmness I had after that talk with God grounded me. I was curious and inspired to learn about this divine intelligence. I'd never read about it before. In fact, at that time, my faith was borderline weak, practically non-existent. I took religion with a pinch of salt.

At that point in time in my life, I was in a very dark place, but I had a realisation that I had to get out of this place. This wasn't my life, and I refused to carry on this way. I needed to take control of my life. I wanted my own vision and goal. None of those things existed, and in my search, I had to answer the deep question of 'Who am I, and where is my identity embedded?'.

The interesting fact that I came across was how to read the Bible. When I asked a friend, 'How do I start reading a Bible?', they said, 'Just start from the beginning'. I thought, 'Oh, that is so lame. Can't you give me some insightful parts where I can go straight and learn immediately about God?'. That was the impatient me.

The person kept on saying, 'No, go back and just read from the first chapter', and I did. I read from the first chapter, and not too far from that Chapter One (verse 26 or so), I had a very big 'Aha!' moment.

Lesson 8: Rediscovering my true self

I read about the creation of everything within seven days. In the last part of this chapter, God said, 'Let us create men in our image, in our likeness', and I thought, 'Why is He saying "Let *us*?"' Then I thought maybe it was a misspelling, or that the version of the Bible I was using was incorrect. I went to search all different kinds of scriptures, and it was the same. 'Let us create men in our own image and likeness'. And I thought; Okay, so if God is saying, 'let us', what happens to the idea of God being God by Himself? Who was with Him now? That is how much I had no idea of the 'Holy Trinity' (*God, the Father, the Son, and the Holy Spirit*). The excitement of being made in his image and likeness *was my unique identity right there.* I found what I was searching for; an answer to my core identity. I needed no more external validations.

My narrow identity of myself was blown away; that of my clan, nationality, family. I understood that God said He is spirit, He poured His spirit unto us (*me*), and He declared that He knows our (*my*) names. I was intrigued by the words, 'I knew you before you were a seed in your mother's womb, I called you by your name'. I didn't doubt this, and it settled on me that I do have a father in heaven.

My parents, bless them, were chosen to bring my soul here. I like that a lot, and it changed my perspective on how I viewed myself. The scriptures refer to how we can't comprehend the depth and width of God's love for us with our limited consciousness.

For the first time, something dropped in my soul and stirred up my spirit from within. There was a gentle, different voice that was speaking to me, saying, 'It is all well', prompting me to ask and seek more. This became my mystery. Well, let me tell you. At this point, my excitement was internal, and I wasn't about to tell anyone about this in case I got judged. This was a weird space for me too, but I was loving the change I felt, the calmness, and the '*knowing*' that came with it. So, I protected this weirdness.

My curiosity led me to discover that there's a whole world I'd never understood about God, a powerful guiding force beyond matter and the physical. There's certainty that we'll undergo life's trials, hardships, and challenges. But we must be of good cheer and attitude as we face the trials of life, as we are designed to overcome them. This knowledge allowed me to embrace a spirit of gratitude amid my hardships. The choice we have is a tough one, and we need blind faith to choose life, positivity, and love towards one another.

That pulled hard at my heartstrings and brought in a level of comfort and soothing that I'd not experienced in a long time. Suddenly, I became confident that I could do this because I had a powerful guiding force. I was a child of God. That was settled in my mind.

Practical tips for daily life

- Who do you say you are? Do you define yourself because you're a mother, a sister, a lover, a son? That's your social identity.
- Or are you a kind, ambitious, and caring person? That speaks to your personality.
- A career person, a businessperson, a teacher? That speaks to your function and your roles.
- It's important that you start to unlock the question of who you are and find the right answer for yourself.

9

SIXTH SENSE

Guiding Force

'You have power over your mind, not outside events.
Realise this and you will find strength.

—MARCUS AURELIUS

The battle is really in the mind. We hear this all the time whenever people try to explain a very complex situation. More than a decade after the passing of my father, I was held to ransom by fear and a very depressed mindset. This really closed me off to any possible positive message for my own good. By divine intervention, I was later open to change.

Lesson 1: Connect identity with inner strength

I guess a breakthrough comes from shattering the container of your own emotional pain. It feels like a release, and fear fades away. As a guiding force, the spirit of infinite intelligence gave me the strength to face my reality. For the first time after what seemed like forever, I started to look up with hope. Amid a storm brewing in my life, I could catch my breath again. The foundational seed that was planted within me when I was a kid began to germinate in this new soil of faith and strength through rediscovering my identity.

Cultivating your inner strength must become your number one focus. This begins with an awareness of your own thoughts and mindset.

Learn the power that lies within your innate intellectual mind to impact you to create a beautiful life. When you understand what's within you, you start to trust the inner strength and inner voice. This gives you the confidence to try new ways of looking at the world around you. And the courage to pursue the goals that you really wanted, but couldn't do in your past because you were held to ransom by fear.

Also, this led to becoming a participant in my own life story rather than watching and drifting on autopilot. The great news is that you already have this inner power within you.

I was in self-discovery mode; I applied myself like I usually do in anything that I must tackle.

Lesson 2: Laying the foundation of trust with the Infinite

In my various roles as an Operations Executive, I was wired to think in terms of process and to analyse data to figure out solutions. I did the same here. I applied myself with the same diligence. One of the first few strength-building acts was that I accepted that I'm a child of God, a spirit being. That was where the basis of my identity was anchored. I'm more than my physical body; an energy connected to the divine source beyond the realms of this physical world.

This was my intuition from all that I'd read and researched. This was the little firm voice that whispers from within, and this is what I chose to follow. I know that there are various references to God, depending on religion, culture, or nationality. People tend to refer to God as a higher power or the Universe or the Cosmos. I accepted 'I am Spirit'. The divine energy is part of who I am. It's part of my breath, and I have this spiritual DNA. I also accepted that the divine presence is there in every moment, be it pain, joy, hardship, or growth. He guides me and is the lamp to my feet; this gives me so much comfort. I can't even begin to tell you what it did in my actual head and heart. My brain probably tried to rationalise, but my heart and mind accepted it. This is what allowed me to breathe in the hope and possibilities. I felt some peace from the onslaught of anxiety, panic, and doubts.

For anyone, it could be a different kind of anchor. You could be connected to the universe, the cosmos, or a higher being. The question is awareness of your source of identity.

Please indulge me here onwards, as I understand it isn't very popular to talk to and about God. It's possible that some readers will say, 'Okay, is this about religion?'. I can assure you; this is far from it. And frankly, I get why there's scepticism on this subject, as religion has put me off in many ways too.

That's also why I was surprised that my encounter with God was outside a church or religious setting. So, please hear me out. Whatever your God or higher power is to you is all right with me, as your identity can be rooted in that.

I'm just sharing my choice, including what changed and moved the needle for me to change my perspective. And I'm not imposing this on anyone else. Also, I do appreciate our diversity in how we experience and express our lives. I just wanted to share how I changed for the better, how it started for me. It's my hope that I can trigger a reflective mindset for someone seeking change in their lives and help them connect with their guiding force.

Lesson 3: The trust strengthens the self

My journey started because I was seeking the truth. This became a spiritual quest for me, as I was trying to understand rather than just follow religion blindly. Because I'd done that before, religion did not make any difference. In fact, it made me pull away and I felt condemned, and that made me feel even worse. But this time, I had a spiritual revelation just by encountering peace and clarity in this quest. In the beginning, I was doubtful; things didn't just fall into place in one fell swoop. I had many conversations with God and my inner voice.

What surprised me was the calmness and quiet engagement, as I was stubborn at first. But I was reassured that He is infinite wisdom and a source of infinite intelligence. His love is unending. With His spirit poured into me, *the energy and essence of Him is within me.* I trusted this and fully believed it. Maybe Carl Jung had a point: there's positive psychological spin from Christianity. It shifted my perspective from negative to positive energy, full of possibilities.

Lesson 4: Gratitude obliterates fear

For the first time, I had self-compassion based on love and grace, and not judgement.

It gave me a moment to be conscious and experience self-appreciation. As I delved into the scriptures, I got a clearer understanding of creation and its intention for me; that I belong in it and that I am worthy. This feeling completely shifted my paradigm of who I thought I was and who I am.

I finally connected with my inner self that's always been there. It felt like I was saying, 'Hello, Holy You' to my real self, the spirit essence in me.

I let go of all the self-limiting beliefs that I had about myself and the people-pleasing trait of trying to fit in, trying to do all kinds of things to please other people. The mask over my life fell away. I felt awakened from the deep conditioning of my ego and social brainwashing. Just encountering the divine essence in me during the spiritual quest changed everything for me, and this is a moment of truth that you too can experience.

Here on earth, we'll face challenges and hardships. This is certain for us all, but we must be strong and confident to know we can overcome these. We have the source of infinite intelligence bestowed upon us and within us through the sound mind that we've been gifted. As I thought about all I've gone through in my life, I realised that I'd also had good moments and pockets of positivity that spurred me to do well.

I completed my undergraduate and master's degree in Business, and did exceptionally well. Whether I was in the corporate world or struck out on my own as an entrepreneur, or as a parent, whatever I wanted to do from the heart seemed to work. These pockets of positivity were there in my life. The negativity mindset created misery and depression. But love, the guiding energy, held me in the moments I became overwhelmed with anxiety. For the sake of my children and my own wellbeing, I had to find lasting transformation for the better, and there had to be more for me.

I knew, at this point, that the grace was the strength, and I was grateful that I was never alone in this pain.

Lesson 5: Power within thoughts

It all started with my thoughts and state of mind. I had the authority to create with the power of thought. And the same goes for you, too: Your state of mind determines your behaviour. For a long time, I'd given up my own values and put others ahead of myself. My thoughts were constantly negative and full of insecurities. The feeling that I wasn't enough, even though I was really hustling, studying, being a dutiful wife, running a business, and trying to be different things to everyone. That was what I created from fear and limiting beliefs.

To alter the outlook of my life, I had to address the grief and the fear. I knew deep down that I needed to shift my perspective, and I found the courage through divine intelligence. The 'how' for me arrived through self-reflection and emotional awareness, together with the courage from the spiritual awakening that nothing was impossible. This was a self-regulating mechanism for me, enabling me to forgive myself for the trap that I'd set myself in a long time ago. It enabled me to change the lens of how I viewed the world through my mind. I guess this is what is meant by 'surrendering' to a higher self.

With this gratitude mindset, I went back to the source of my pain through meditation. I came to terms with the fact that it wasn't my fault how adults handled and supported my grief as a young child. Also, it wasn't my fault how I later made bad choices out of insecurities that ended in a bad relationship. I wasn't tuning into my intuition at the time, but I had to forgive and let go. This came through many conversations with God through prayer, journaling, and meditation. I recognised I was a mess, and there was no way I was able to contribute positive energy to any relationship at the time. This is the scarcity mindset, a negative energy motivated by fear of the unknown.

As broken people, we tend to aimlessly drift into relationships motivated by the spirit of fear. And then have families. We become broken parents who create a vicious circle within communities. If we're unable to have awareness of ourselves and our identities and don't become mindful of our thoughts, we continue to fester and linger in pain and depression.

No good ever comes out of this state of mind. You, too, can pause and have compassion for your mistakes, bad choices, the hurt others did to you, and pain suffered.

For this, thoughts are powerful. The clarity was that I was not just a mother or a wife or a sister or a single parent or a corporate executive or an entrepreneur or whatever my tradition called me, but an individual spirit first. I was Victoria, the child of the divine and infinite intelligence who experiences life and has a place at the table. This gave me the inner confidence of that eleven-year-old me to rediscover my creative imagination, courage and faith.

Lesson 6: Finding self-worth

I also began to develop self-reliance that enabled me to centre my thoughts, and this gave me the contentment of knowing that I'm good enough. I had a purpose in life, and I had self-worth. It became a crucial shift for me to move forward and lift my spirits. Suddenly, I was calm, and the anxious thoughts or negativity dissipated. I guess this is what 'peace that surpasses all understanding' means.

This spiritual awakening gave me a positive outlook more than anything else. I was able to meditate quietly without panic. I was able to view myself without judgement, while taking responsibility that some of the 'bad' in my life resulted from my own thoughts. I was learning to move forward, with the spirit of self-compassion leading me.

And the key element for me was I was able to forgive others for whatever they did or what I thought they did to me.

And that gave me a release and freedom that was refreshing and liberating.

In my research and spiritual quest, the scriptures found in 2 Timothy 1:7, *'For God did not give us a spirit of fear, but he has given us a spirit of power and of love and sound mind'* made me curious. *A spirit of power and sound mind.* I'm a person who loves to understand what things mean. If I were to start a business or any project, I must have clarity of intentions, and clarify the purpose so that I have a strong, compelling reason for it. The start was my identity, and I anchored all my faith on divine wisdom and intelligence.

To gain different perspectives, my practical side kicked in. I began to research deeply. In my undergraduate studies, I majored in psychology. This created a fascination with the psyche, neuroscience, and all related subjects. When I stumbled on the phrase, *'I've given you sound mind'*, I took it as a definition of abilities that result in a calm, well-balanced mind, self-control, and a power to act on it.

Lesson 7: Refine your perspectives

I pondered words, marvelling that *you can call things that are not as though they are.* And this allows you to go into what we now call visualisation. You can visualise things that are not as though they are, using power of thoughts. The ability to see your desires, think about your future, and go into this ability of using meditation, imagination, and visualisation.

I spent some time reviewing science of the mind and how neuroscience impacts our abilities to create our new reality.

Evidence from published journals clearly explain that our own thoughts are powerful enough to manifest whatever we think. This was a big deal to me, because now this wasn't just about religion in the background. It became a spiritual quest that somehow overlapped with a scientific outlook. Scientists like Dr Bruce H Lipton and Leonard Mlodinow have shared their consensus that conscious thoughts are powerful and that the subconscious mind rules our behaviour.

Lesson 8: The subconscious mind works behind the scenes

I'm not a scientist, but by reading many books and peer-reviewed journals, I discovered supporting material to confirm that our thoughts impact us deeply. There's even an old saying: *You are what you think.*

Most of us don't think we have control over our thoughts. In the past, I felt the same way. However, the Bible says ask for something, and believe you've received it, then give thanks. That is the process for our dreams to manifest. It starts from our thoughts.

How many of us are doing that? And how many of us think that we can't control our thoughts? Are you one of those people who think that your thoughts are random, that you don't have any input in manifesting your thoughts? To my surprise, I can control my thoughts with practice and awareness. I know you can too. *But do we?*

The fact is, you and I have been created with power and sound mind. This is a gift, whether it's from the universe, the cosmos, or a higher power. For me, it's from God the creator.

Lesson 9: Inside the Black Box

Starting with the body, the physical aspect of our being includes all our organs and brain where the rational consciousness resides. I call this the human supercomputer, the fascinating brain organ. Our thought impulses start right here in our conscious mind. The impulses are inputs from our external and internal data using our cognitive abilities. That's then processed by the rational mind to produce a thought or an idea, which could be a negative or a positive thought.

What are your thoughts about, especially if you think your thoughts are random and you can't control them, or that your environment influences your thoughts? The question then is: What are you manifesting with your thoughts? Is it what you want or desire?

Energy flows from the spirit of infinite intelligence. Science claims that our organs are controlled by this part involuntarily (*your organs right now work without your permission or interference, like your heartbeat*), that is, the subconscious or subjective mind. I like to call it energy flow (I picture it as electricity flow). Now, science (*quantum field theory*) also indicates that the universe has energy and all its creation from atoms that control the flow of energy, which creates waves of vibration (*Big Think journal*).

Vibrations of energy at the right frequency levels can manifest and change things in our lives. I find a similar scripture in Gallatians 5:22—that the creator is Spirit, the source of life, and is yet invisible to mankind. We can come to Him in Spirit within and truthful worship.

With these insights, I had a compelling reason to pursue the design of my own life. The new understanding was instrumental in manifesting the life I wanted. It wasn't up to someone else—my family, my friends, my partner, my spouse, my children, or my culture. It was up to me. This was formulated from my thoughts and my state of mind, and how I reacted and responded to my external environment.

The limiting beliefs came to a halt once I understood that I was in control and had inner strength. This was a spiritual awakening, as a positive attitude enabled me to follow what to think about. To cut off the random thoughts, I intentionally thought of all that was honourable and worthy of respect; whatever was right, wholesome, lovely, and brought peace in all my daily experiences. These activities retained the newfound calmness, and a move away from the fearful mindset. I made time to learn more about the character and essence of the infinite intelligence.

As I journaled the thoughts of my desires, motivated by the advice to 'call things that are not as though they are', using my faith and visualisation, I had clarity. This was not a religious factor, either. I wasn't trying to please others, but was doing this for myself for the first time since my adolescent years. I knew this wasn't fashionable at all. The motivation came because it gave me peace and harmony that I couldn't find anywhere else in the world.

I couldn't find it in a church, with friends, or in paid professional roles.

That gave me this constant positivity, which gave me courage. I'm more than my physical body; I'm part of creation and have a sound mind. I didn't have to bow down to cultural judgement and social demands. Instead, I found the courage to accept that I was my own person, and I was unapologetic about it. I wasn't being arrogant. It was a process of rediscovering my confidence.

The scriptures say in Hebrews 10:35, 'Don't throw away your confidence *[fearless]*, for it has great reward.' These thought inputs changed my perspective. People said, 'Oh, you're different. Something about you has changed'. I felt calmer, and I was more compassionate towards myself, but I was also more compassionate to other people. I became a tolerant person, but not a pushover.

Lesson 10: Change creates a domino effect

This 'new me' impacted my corporate executive role and leadership style, and I became more compassionate and patient with others. The results were astonishing: My teams worked in harmony to produce value as my positive energy spread into them. My state of mind became contagious.

Prior to this, I was clinical and demanding. I was a leader who pushed and pushed without taking a break. I was overworking as a means of closing the emotional void. But this gave me a new sense of purpose. I became a different mother. I had quality time with my children, which I never seemed to have before. In the previous emotional dispensation, as I call it, I was constantly pushing myself on life's treadmill because I had this scarcity mindset. I was afraid I was going to lose something. I was afraid I had to work harder as a single parent because I had to provide for my children. I had to make sure that I didn't lose those material things. All this anxiety and stress came to an end.

From the moment I understood I had the inner strength, and that I could attract all the good in my life, I finally understood that I didn't have to chase things. They would come to me. Yes, they will come to me. 'Seek first the kingdom of God and all these *things* will be added unto you', say the scriptures as written in Matthew 6:33. I figured that the Kingdom of Heaven is within me, not in a church or any religion. The things to be added to you start with your thoughts, your sound mind, and your beliefs that manifest your persistent desire.

I was considerate, compassionate, and empathetic towards my children. I realised that I'd been hurting my children without even knowing it because I was a busy mom and because my stressful life was full of negativity and self-limiting beliefs. When you're obsessed with pain and burdens, you pay little attention to your children or family. A child comes to you and says, 'Mom, let's do this'. But you rarely have quality time for the child. I was busy over-working myself and was always anxious or stressed about something.

But the inner strength in me, the life energy in me, gave me a new footing and uplifted me. I had to make sure that I didn't lose this beautiful calmness I'd found. I realised that I had to cultivate it and make it a new habit for myself.

In hindsight, all the detours in my life became a blessing. Even the pain, distress, and abuse that I experienced were blessings in disguise, because I hadn't known that something in me was being made whole at the time. Once I recognised I was overcoming the pressures of my life, I had newfound strength, and I began to cultivate the philosophy of 'this too shall pass' when I was confronted with stressful and hard moments.

The strength and confidence grew from the realisation that *I had overcome that.* I am sure you must have had moments that were challenging in your life, and you overcame them one at a time. But for some reason, we tend to keep all the negative parts of our lives, rather than all the beautiful parts that we've overcome. For me, those are the stepping stones to discovering that you're stronger than what you give yourself credit for. You're more than your limiting beliefs, and you are enough. Only you can start showcasing the positive energy you embody, and let it spread to those around you.

Therefore, you must focus on the goodness and solutions in you and not the problem. Focus on the fact that you're good enough to navigate this life with the gift inside you, your essence, and that inner voice that guides you to overcome whatever hardships you face.

Think about the ideas or desires for your life—and then believe, engaging all your senses. This way, your conscious mind is activated, creating instruction for your subconscious mind, that energy that delivers results.

Awareness is being mindful of your state of mind as it aligns with your dreams and desires. You must be intentional; you must be resolute that this is who I am now. You must be filled with a sound mind and belief in yourself. Focus on harnessing and building your mental resilience so you can counter adversity in your life. Let's check out the building blocks.

Practical tips for everyday life

- A breakthrough comes from shattering the container of your own emotional pain. Then, it really feels like a release, and fear fades away.
- Rediscovering your identity is where your inner strength lies. Cultivating this must become your Number One focus. And it begins with an awareness of your own thoughts.
- Awareness is being mindful of your state of mind as it aligns with your dreams and desires.
- We have the source of infinite intelligence bestowed on us and within us through the sound mind that we've been gifted.
- Know that 'this too shall pass' when you face hardships.

10

MENTAL RESILIENCE

Believing in the Belief Itself

*'Most people think faith means believing in
something. Often it means trying something,
giving it a chance to prove itself.'*

—HENRY FORD, 1922

*W*ho *said life was fair?* We've all heard this old saying in response to hardships. It's certain that adversities will happen at some point in one's life, and at the centre of that is one's own thoughts of how to overcome them. So, are you taking captive every thought that's a stronghold in your life? Are you tackling the thought that prevents you from being your truest self? Are you being hijacked by fear-based thoughts or a scarcity mindset?

By the end of this chapter, you'll appreciate the awareness of your essence, your true self-identity, and its importance in redirecting your thought impulse to mental resilience. Success in anything one attempts requires a resilient mindset that's based on one's belief system.

Lesson 1: Building blocks of resilience

The journey to mental toughness starts with cultivating your innate strength and rediscovering your self-identity. What are the thoughts and positive beliefs in your abilities to overcome adversities that life throws at you? Mental strength is what assists you in remaining focused under pressure and refusing to be intimidated by your circumstances.

Believing in the belief itself is where it all starts. As mentioned earlier, everything in our life is dependent on the quality of our state of mind. Are you a person who worries about everything and sees failure before you begin anything? Or are you a hopeful type of person with a can-do attitude, having a positive outlook on anything you embark on?

Science and spirituality experts seem to agree that thoughts have the power to create. And furthermore, what one believes has a great impact on their behaviour. Given this view, pause and think about what mostly occupies your thoughts. Observe the thoughts; don't deny them; they could be positive or negative. You don't want this impact to be random or surprise you. With my curious mindset, some of my findings are that thoughts are impulses that start from our conscious mind. The impulses can come from various external and internal factors, such as your upbringing, your memories, your family, your current location, where you grew up, your nationality, your education, or the news. It could be social media, or it could be your friends.

Input can also come from the energy of the five senses. This includes sight, touch, smell, taste, and sound. For the time being, let's call these inputs into your rational mind. This is where you process the impulses, formulate a thought or idea. and make decisions. Choose what you're going do with it.

When I was an eleven-year-old, in hindsight, I had a child-like faith. I trusted my father. I believed in the belief itself. It wasn't about the activities with my father, but it was just believing it. I just accepted it without a doubt. I'm sure you've heard of a father asking a two-year-old daughter to jump from a table or high place into his arms. The reaction of the child, if there's no one interfering with this, is to just jump into the arms of the father. There are no external influences, but total trust.

The child has no concept of fear. This freedom is also referred to as childlike faith. Believing thrives in a socially supportive environment, which was what I felt with my father. Children have innate faith in their parents, that they'll catch them when they jump. This is belief.

It's important to define your truth for yourself, settle this in your mind, and lay a foundation of trust. When all the input from within and external factors confront you, you must make a choice. And that's the only responsibility aligned directly with the designed life outcome you seek. Our rational mind collects data from our environment and within, processes it, then takes a decision. Once a choice is made, it's sent for delivery to the subconscious mind, your soul, the energy force that's within you.

Lesson 2: Choice for the self

I believe that I'm a spirit being, that I possess a soul that houses my subconscious mind and have a body that's the physical aspect of who I am, with all my rational conscious mind in there. I shared earlier that my breakthrough was founded on an understanding of the fundamental connection to my identity. Therefore, believing is a choice that one has to make one way or another. Anyone who comes to Him must believe that He does exist and rewards those who diligently seek Him, says the scriptures.

Let's try this. I'm sure you've sat on a chair many times. You probably walked into a room for the first time, and it was full of strangers or other people. And you had to sit on a chair.

You don't ask other people that are seated if the chair's safe to sit; you simply sit. This has become normal for us. I know this is also a very simplistic way of looking at things, but I'm trying to drive home a point about believing in the belief itself.

In the example of the chair, you don't question anything. It becomes certain that you know what you know. Let's try another one. Hopefully, when you read this, your heart's beating at seventy beats per minute for an adult and a bit higher for a child. Have you perhaps ever met your heart or your brain, lungs, or kidneys? Any of your organs? Hopefully, only if you're a surgeon or medical professional. Even these medical heroes can't see their organs, which is amazing, isn't it?

So, it would be fair to say your unique fingerprint is one of a kind, in a world of more than eight billion people.

A well-respected scientist, former medical professor, Dr H Leptin, confirms in his writing that human beings have one of the most complex physiologies that synchronises and works in harmony by design. How do you explain that? The science fraternity can't even explain how this body of ours functions automatically.

Lesson 3: You're perfect as you are

You're set apart; you're loved unconditionally. You have new mercies every single day. Whatever you put your mind to, you can achieve. And this is my belief, as it's happened to me several times in my life.

The question to ask is: Have you checked your belief lately? Are you believing fully in your desires and dreams? Are your thoughts aligned with your beliefs? If not, maybe it's time to investigate the part of you that still doubts. Accepting who you are is a decision only *you* can make. No amount of persuasion can change this. This is informed by what you tell yourself about yourself, because change comes from within. I understood from many readings that life really boils down to a few things, and one of them is choice. We make decisions all the time.

If you think negatively about who you are and have self-limiting beliefs, this would be your main obstacle in achieving your truest self.

Your thoughts are crucial to your choice, but you must know first who you are. What's the basis for your identity? Is it compelling enough for you to start believing in it? It's said that the subconscious mind rules our behaviour and actions, and uses information from our conscious mind. The interesting thing is that the subconscious mind is a servant of the conscious mind. It doesn't make jokes, rationalise, or decide.

The subconscious mind executes on the demand of the boss, our conscious mind. And what spiritual intelligence says about creation is that the battle is within the mind and that belief is the key fundamental shift to a fulfilled, purposeful life. If you believe with your heart and say it with your mouth, it will be done. Those are the ancient teachings. The whole brain–mind integration process is to effectively communicate personal goals to the subconscious where they'll be delivered. In my case, becoming an entrepreneur to lead a staff of employees and run an organisation required the confidence of a woman who's not marred by the past. The identity of the past no longer exists.

The identity you eventually choose is what matters in reaching your authentic self or North Star.

I'd reached a crossroads in my relationship when it was either everyone else's happiness or my own. I either had to stay miserable in the Hell I'd created in my mind, be a passive people-pleaser, and watch my life from the sidelines. Or I could take the reins of my life and be a full participant in designing my destiny.

It works in the world of science and spirituality. They may be worlds apart; however, they've provided us with an understanding of how our minds control our behaviour, and eventually our destiny.

Lesson 4: The knowledge within is Titanic

Some of you might recall the very successful 1997 movie *Titanic,* with actors Leonardo DiCaprio and Kate Winslet in a love story that ended in a tragic manner. The movie brought to light some interesting analogies with our minds.

The *Titanic* was a luxury ship on a maiden voyage to America. This ship had all the bells and whistles of a luxury cruise liner. Travellers ranged from the wealthy to those seeking to change their lives. The story to me is likened to how the mind works.

As I explained to my mentees and those under my leadership, I had an understanding of how the conscious and subconscious mind influences and rules our behaviour, and how important it is to be mindful of our thoughts and our inputs (Mlodinow, L 2012). The movie tells the story of this grand ship led by a very experienced captain on his last voyage before retiring. He'd be gathering all information from his manager or junior captains in the upper stern and from the boiler room. Based on all this information, he'd decide and give instructions on how to proceed. So, he kept an eye on what was happening in all the areas, including his own experience. I liken this to the two hemispheres of our mind. The Captain, which is like your conscious or rational part, instructs the Stern Captain to go at a certain rate or speed up or to slow down. The Deck Captain shouts out this command to the guys below in the boiler room; these are the guys who add coal to ensure that the engine is running smoothly.

I liken the boiler engine to the subconscious mind.

The interesting part is that those boilers fuelling the ship to float or speed ahead simply follow instructions. They don't question or challenge the orders given to them. So, the tragedy ensued, unfortunately. This was the result of the external inputs or influence on the Captain, the conscious mind. He was persuaded, against his own better judgement and years of experience, to speed up so he could give reporters the news that they'd arrived early.

This part relates to how most of us know what we need to do through intuition. This is your inner voice telling you that this was the wrong or right decision, and your experience would tell you the same thing, too.

However, the intuition gets ignored at times. You go against your better judgement because you want to please people. You don't want to create conflict. Some say, '*I don't want to rock the boat*'. You don't want to stand out; you want to belong or fit in. So, we go along with the flow, but we're internally in turmoil and regret follows afterwards. The same was true for the captain of the *Titanic*.

Not a single person in the boiler room questioned the change of decision. They could see that there were icebergs, and they knew there was a risk hitting one of these icebergs. They were to cruise according to the schedule, and they continued as instructed. This is the part of our minds that doesn't rationalise or make decisions. This part just observes, takes our good or limiting beliefs as truth; and executes and delivers, even if it's to our own detriment.

Lesson 4: Solution-oriented self-talk

In the everyday decision-making process, what do you believe in that is working for you? Are you aware of your self-talk? Is it supportive of what you want for yourself?

I recall how my father used positive affirmations in coaching my brother. His positive self-talk of intended outcome became the culture in his camp. Are you spending time thinking about what you want, or are you spending time thinking about what you can't have? Do you have misconceptions about certain people, that they can't rise to a certain level of success?

Are you focusing more on the problem than the solution?

Part of building resilience is focusing on identifying the challenge or adversity, acknowledging its pain points or difficulties, and thinking of mitigating or finding the 'silver lining' in every situation.

As a single mom, I realised I had serious challenges ahead of me. It was like starting over in every sense. But I had to be optimistic and realistic about what I could do in the short term. It was important to have a plan in place. This fuelled my motivation, and suddenly, the obstacles were not so 'impossible' or overwhelming. I believed I could do this. I believed in my abilities and, perhaps more importantly, that I was not alone—*I had infinite wisdom and a sound mind.*

If you create thoughts, which of these thoughts are aligned to your North Star, your burning desire? Are you aware of what unconscious data you're gathering, and how it influences your state of mind?

When you're a worrisome type of person, worry, obviously, will be the outcome you get. When you're confident of being victorious, then victory is what you're going to get. There are acceptable levels of worry one needs in order to activate all the right hormones and be ready to enter into a mode of being productive. But then there's the excessive one, where you're sitting there, paralysed by worry and anxiety. The latter one, when excessive and prolonged, moves someone into depression. It starts to affect you physiologically. Applying a solution-oriented mindset that believes that all problems can be resolved is the best. Fear can paralyse the decision-making process, but it can be talked through. That's where self-talk can be the solution.

The only way to banish fear is to believe that you're purposefully made by the creator and that you're meant to be here; that you have a contribution to make, and you're worthy. You're created with an innate ability to navigate the trials of life without losing your joy because of the resilience inside you. Believing you're special, that you matter, and that nothing's impossible because of the infinite intelligence and wisdom within you, is a starting point for you to thrive—you must first choose to believe and have expectancy.

Whatever you base your belief on is all on you. With self-compassion, I was able to let go of my past, forgive myself, and forgive others as well. Owning my story meant freedom, which became the absence of fear. I realised that I'd overcome so much in my past and never took time to appreciate and acknowledge my own growth. I then redirected my thoughts, away from scarcity mindset, to that of enough available resources to lead me to prosperity, this relates to my belief in the abundance mindset.

This gave me renewed hope and gratitude to face all the facets of my life. All the trials that I experienced in my life had brought me to a certain point of awareness and of immense gratitude. I rewarded myself; self-appreciation was necessary in order to move forward. This renewed my commitment as I kept on pushing the boundaries of my own creative imagination fearlessly. With this persistence and purpose, my confidence grew. I was already resilient, but not mentally resilient enough to be able to repeat this with absolute belief. I then became resolute to change the negative conversations within my thoughts to positive affirmations. Success in life or in business, or for anything you seek at all, needs mental toughness. I watched this with my father and all the boxers that he trained. That important factor was not just the physical training, but the mental resilience.

Lesson 5: Find your recipe for success

The formula for success, as per the scriptures, is to meditate on the word day and night and to ponder on the wisdom. Don't let this out of your mind. Pondering pushes us to think. Meditation requires calmness and quietness, and you go deep into yourself; you cut out all the noise and the chatter in the world. In the quiet moments, you listen to the divine wisdom guiding you. I had to use my imagination and visualisation to enable me to start. I began with an end in mind, by asking myself what kind of life I wanted. I was very specific about it, what it really included, and why. I engaged my full senses and my imagination, up to the minute details of where and what the end results would be. *Who is with me during this time, and what colours do I see? What is the ambience? What do I smell, hear, taste, see and feel?* Just engaging all my senses in whatever it is that I put my mind to in the visualisation process was the aim. And in the calmness, the responses, conversations, and guidance will be crystal-clear. This will ignite a passion that's undeterred by external views of whatever I decided as my target goal.

I'd have vivid dreams about actions or people, and this would actually happen. If I have a dream about meeting a person or seeking certain resources, I'd end up experiencing some of that.

Somehow, the resources would come and solve some of the puzzles and problems I was going through at any point in time. As these events happened to me, I became confident that I could do this and that this was the right process.

For example, I was standing in McDonald's Times Square in 1993 or thereabouts. I'd gone on a trip, and at the time was a corporate worker, but an entrepreneur in spirit. I looked at a particular company's business and thought, 'Wow, this is a huge and global business'. The brand hadn't arrived in South Africa (SA) at the time. Fast forward to 1996. I was travelling as an executive for an executive programme at Cambridge University, United Kingdom. In the programme, I was pleasantly surprised to be working on a McDonald's business case. It was like the universe was nudging me to my earlier thoughts of wanting to own such a business.

And the urge this time was much stronger. I came back and communicated to my family that I would investigate opening a McDonald's. At that time, in 1995, business was liberalising in South Africa. I journaled that I'd one day own one of these stores. I wrote that I'd have a 'Mac-destiny'. As they say, when a vision is given to you, others won't see it. So, in 1996, I tried to get into McDonald's, but I was told that they weren't taking in any franchisees at the time. I was in my late twenties. I still think the person I spoke to on the other side of the phone probably thought I was too young and wouldn't know how to manage a brand name.

There were a few McDonald's in South Africa at the time, but being rejected didn't stop my pursuit. I was persistent in seeking a global entity that had a strong brand presence to partner with. I did all the research into franchising, and had unsuccessful ventures. But these failed attempts didn't deter me. The vision had been planted in my soul and I wasn't letting it go. I continued to chase the dream and went to other brands, like British Petroleum and Chicken Licken (a local fast-food restaurant). That was how I cut my teeth in the global franchising space.

A few years later, I tried again after completing my Master of Business Administration, and harvested those businesses. I spent some time in banking, working with two of the big major banks in South Africa as an executive in services and in operations. I had a detour, but it was all grace that enabled me to develop the experiences that were important. So, all roads were leading me to becoming a global brand franchisee.

It's my passion now to share my experiences, mentoring others who face similar challenges.

What impulse or input influences your mind?

What do you allow as a rational truth to you, and what do you believe in?

Whatever the answer to these questions is would be your life story. When you overcome things in your past, you learn what and why you succeeded, and why you can't do the same things again. I'll share with you why I'm able to go through many challenges without them tearing my spirit. It's because now, I'm focused on mental resilience training.

I'm making choices that are beneficial to me and those around me. The more I practised controlling my thoughts, aligning them to my North Star, and the more action I took, the better progress I seemed to make. This gave me the confidence and courage that I could consistently overcome struggles and not be intimidated by the next hurdle.

This means that you, too, can rediscover your potential and develop a consistent habit, making progress with small actions and wins that are cumulative. This way, you take control of your own story. For me, it was believing in my dreams and gaining the positive outlook founded on my identity. I was intentional and committed to continuous improvement of my lot, irrespective of my circumstances. As much as this gave me momentum to progress forward, it was far from the end. The most critical shift happened when I focused on my habits. This was my game-changer.

Practical tips for everyday life

- Solution-oriented self-talk leads to positive outcomes.
- Intuition provides answers, so listen through meditation and calmness.
- Trust that there's a guiding power that will lead you to succeed.
- All roads lead to the achievement of your North Star.
- Be resilient and never let failures be a deterrent.

11

HABITUAL THINKING

Practice Makes Progress

*'It's not what we do once in a while that shape our
lives, but what we do consistently.'*

—Tony Robbins

We're all creatures of habit, good or bad. The question is: Why does it seem easier to repeat bad habits and much harder to repeat good ones? Why is this so difficult?

The answer lies in the transformation process from your identity to what you want to do, the meaning and value you attach, and how you're going to get there. On reflection, I'm sure there was something in your life that you once thought was tough or was a big challenge that looked like an insurmountable problem.

It could have been a difficult assignment, a new project, letting go of a toxic relationship, or just starting afresh. But, somehow, you surprised yourself, faced it, and moved forward. The residue of this tribulation and trials lingers on from our past. This is what makes most of us seek more out of life and know that something isn't quite right.

Unknowingly, we overcame these challenges in the past, but we want to remove the residual stuff from lingering in our minds negatively. Making a clean break from it all will give you that extra lift to face new challenges and any demands that life throws at us. Thoughts are powerful, and awareness of these thoughts can lead to better habits. It's your responsibility to change your thoughts so you can align to what *you* want, not what *others* want. This is the main theme of this book. Think about what you're thinking about, so you can build new habits and own your life story. Take charge of your thoughts, rewrite your story, and break the ceiling of your own self-limiting beliefs.

Lesson 1: Seek resolution

Settle in your mind who you are. Be resolute in transforming yourself to live your most purposeful life. There's power in knowing your identity, your essence, and your spirit, and not just your different roles. This starts with believing in the belief itself, that you're enough, and resilient enough, to harness the power of the divine infinite intelligence and wisdom within you.

Having a resolute mindset gives you direction. This fuels passion for change within and gives purpose to waking up every morning.

Habits are crucial in this. Habit forms a basis for a routine or practice that leads to inner strength. One more thing: Habits are hard to give up. A habit is a learned behaviour rather than an innate thing. We all have behaviours; we choose them.

The quality of our lives depends on the quality of habits we discipline ourselves to maintain. So, the operative word here is quality. Once the habit's ingrained, it takes little or no effort; it becomes routine; it becomes a thinking default. The question is, 'Whatever habits you have right now, are they effective to produce your desires?'.

Post-divorce, as a young single mother to children of school age, I had to be resolute in my mind that I was going to be undeterred in being authentic to myself, for me and for my children. And the reason was compelling enough to inspire the confidence for me to transform.

Lesson 2: Life account

Being an Operations Executive came in handy when I started to do strategic planning for my life as a single mother. I wanted to ensure that my children and family were taken care of. This later became my vision board, or what I called my life account.

Why a life account? With an entrepreneurial mindset, my life became an account; there are income and outflows, profitability and losses. Key elements to think about were: 'What was coming into my life?', and 'What was I expending?'. If any area of your life is in debt, as per your own evaluation, that tells you pretty much that you can't do much for yourself or others in this regard. I call it a life account.

I looked at my health and said, 'What do I want for it?'. If it was in a minus or a positive state with respect to my plans, I had to think about what I needed to do. I had to be methodical and bring in all the value chains of my life.

Yes, at the time, I didn't know any other way. My skills and competencies came to the fore to resolve the problem I was confronted with. I crafted this plan to include six to eight life account areas, ranking them from what I thought were the most important to the least impactful.

My life account areas

1. Spirituality
2. Health
3. Wealth and Finances
4. Family and Relationships
5. Business and Career
6. Travel and Adventure
7. Service and Gratitude

So, interestingly, the Bible says you must write your vision and make it plain upon the tablet, so that whoever has to read it may run with it. I began with an end in mind. I thought about the kind of life and quality I desired for myself and my family.

I mentioned that I trusted God, and there's a saying that says, 'Faith without works is dead'. There must be effort applied in order to get results, and this must be persistent. A habit's a good place to start once you know what you want. The key for me was to prioritise and break things up into small goals so that I could execute them. Having spent time in operations and service environments in retails, big corporations, and even my own businesses, I thought about the process. So, you must have an endgame, and it's best to break things into small chunks so that you can execute and cumulatively get to the same goal. This is how I looked at life and was wired.

As someone who had a new lease on life, I could relatively breathe and recognise my own blessing, and I was grateful to be alive. Gratitude became my daily ritual, morning and evening. With this confidence of small wins, I had the courage to find bigger ones. The universe was holding my hand.

Lesson 3: Mental wellbeing matters

Let me share how I took charge of one of the areas in my life account—health.

As someone coming from a stressful, depressed, and anxious mindset, I knew I needed to focus on my recovery, my wellbeing, and mostly my mental wellness.

One of the reasons I wrote this book, using my life experiences, is to create awareness about the importance of mental wellness. I started out with an honest evaluation of my current situation. This was for my own good. You aren't trying to impress anyone when you do this. However, you must be honest with yourself. That is the only way you can notice the gaps between where you are and where you want to be. This was where the small goals come in. This revealed I had huge gaps to work on.

My health vision was that by His stripes, I was healed, and that I'm blessed with a sound mind. This was my core belief for this area, and an attitude and outlook I took. However, for a healthy mental state of mind, I first had to take care of my body.

I made a list of action points to focus on. Here are some examples:

1 Annual medical checks
2 Regular doctor checkups
3 Make time to go to the gym, specifically three times a week
4 Balanced home-cooked meals
5 Vitamin supplements
6 Weekend walks with my kids
7 Adequate sleep of at least seven hours
8 Water hydration. (I had a no juice rule in the house to instil a water-drinking habit in the children.)

Look at this list; it felt impossible. However, small action steps are all it took. I took the first step by registering at the gym. I got a trainer for a few months so I could gain momentum and guidance. Walks in the park included quality time with my children. For sleep, I set my alarm to go to bed at the same time every day. This took a while. I realised that a TV in my bedroom was a distraction, so I took it out. The good outcome of this plan was that my children also learned from my habits and adopted them, too.

Gratitude time was also a daily habit I introduced under the family life account. In the evenings, at 8.30 p.m., we'd say what we were grateful for during that day. Everyone had to think about it and share.

As a single mom, I knew that I wasn't the only one with a distressed past. The divorce impacted the kids just as much as it did me. One of my goals in my life account plan was to learn the Bible's kind of spirituality. I needed family therapy, something to give us all hope. So, every Wednesday night, we had a reading and discussion session. I recall that my son would slouch in his chair, showing he was uninterested, tired and bored. But we soldiered on until he was the one doing the reading with a change of heart.

Even now, as adult children, they still read the Bible on their own. It was a habit we started together. This wasn't being religious, but it gave structure and calm to our family, which was important when I was on my spiritual quest. My children turned out to be respectful, kind children.

I didn't allow violent movies to be watched on television at home. This spoke to my spiritual quest and my understanding of science and neuroscience that our five senses do feed our conscious mind, and that this violence gets imprinted on our subconscious mind. These were negative images I didn't want my children to see, and I didn't want them in my own head either. As they say, a horror movie will scare you long after the movie is finished. The fear can be retained in your mind, and I didn't want that for them. I explained to everyone in my family why I was doing it. And fortunately, the kids were young enough to agree with me, so that it soon became a habit in our home and in our daily lives.

Lesson 4: Mindfulness is a habit

Are you mindful of the habits that are taking place in your home, especially with young children and young adults with access to information and television? Are you aware of the habits they're now starting to learn?

Making what's familiar (self-limiting) unfamiliar so you can instil positive habits is where we want to be. You're probably asking me what I mean by this. Well, *fear,* for example, is False Evidence Appearing Real, made up by the mind. This can be familiar to people because it gives them a reason and a justification for behaving in a certain way. It's a comfortable place that people belong to because they don't know how to break away from it. We want to make this unfamiliar to us and replace it with strength. Faith empowers and can replace fear, because it gives you hope. Faith requires action; this comes from well-thought-out plans from your deep desires. It's your outlook in life and what you believe in. This is how we can reprogramme ourselves and start new habits.

One of the lessons from my life journey was that I wasn't fixated on *how* I was going to achieve the extraordinary life. I was powered by the unshakable *what* I was doing and *why* I was doing it. This was a compelling reason enough for me. I was focused on the solution rather than dwelling on the issue or problem. This is how creative imagination allows you to dream and connect with the spirit gift in you. You can start at any time in your life journey. That is the beauty of being committed to participating in your own life story. Also, habits can be started at any point. You just have to make a decision that you've had enough of a mediocre life. As long as you've got an awareness that you want to change your life story, you can start at any point.

There's extensive literature showing that habit-forming behaviour requires consistency and repetition to reinforce—the behaviour of regularity. The daily habits become ingrained and require little to no effort or thought later. This is when the new habit becomes familiar, and you've reprogrammed yourself to start. Momentum is key to solidifying your actions and seeing them through to fruition.

The critical part, though, is to check if whatever habit you have is aligned to your North Star and if it's productive to your desires. When I think back to my eleven-year-old self and how my dad trained boxers, I realised that was habit-forming behaviour.

My brother would be at the gym every day in the afternoon. His physical training included running over thirty kilometres in the mornings at 5 a.m. and swimming at different intervals on different days. This was the norm for him and it became a habit. By being close to my dad, I ended up waking at 5 a.m. in the mornings as well. Even at weekends, I'm still up at dawn. It's a habit I picked up when I was young.

Interestingly, my siblings never woke up that early. They hated it. Even on school days, they would wake up an hour before they had to go to school. I would have been up a few hours earlier, getting ready and having my quality time with Dad.

This indicates how we choose and accept input that comes at us and how that, in turn, influences our decisions.

In my career and businesses, whenever I decided on something and I intentionally put it into practice, it somehow worked out for me. Some say it's luck. But my father used to say, 'You make your own luck.' I guess with habit, repetition being the mother of all learning, you can make your own luck. It is only through practice that one gets it right. Practice makes progress. You must take the first step.

Practical tips for everyday life

- The question is: Why is it easier to repeat bad habits, and much harder to repeat good ones?
- When we overcome challenges in our past, we need to remove the negative residue still lingering in our minds.
- At every step, thoughts are powerful, and awareness that your thoughts create your current life is crucial.
- Identity matters when it comes to breaking the ceiling of your own self-limiting beliefs.
- Create a life account. Then, take one small action to change it for the better.
- Check in with your feelings. A sense of excitement and positivity means you're aligned to your North Star.

CONCLUSION

Self-mastery accepts failure—
Victoria Moya

I hear from my mentees, 'When is the right time to start?'
My answer is: 'Always, there's never one right time. Just start'. As motion alters your emotions, this gives you momentum. Even failure teaches you something. I've had failures in my start-ups, but this has given me lots of insights and prepared me for coming opportunities. When I look back, it's been the failures that have contributed most to my resilience do-over. It was that spirit of not giving up, falling and dusting yourself off, reviewing what you might have missed, and going at it again. There are lots of learnings from failure; if we just take the time and not complain or shift blame, we can learn.

To action change, you must be fed up with your current situation and want more because you know you deserve more. You must be open to the change and disciplined enough to follow your inner voice that tells you that you must take certain actions. Being clear on my reality and having self-awareness of where I was and where I wanted to be, the gap was very clear. The life account plan kickstarts the momentum to achieve dreams.

With a solution-finding mindset or growth mindset, there was no time to complain. With each small goal achieved, confidence grew, which in turn spurred me on. I intuitively knew I was on the right track. I felt it in my physiology, that feeling of excitement and of the confident young Victoria—she was back.

The scriptures say, 'Do not, therefore fling away your confidence [boldness], for it has great reward'- Hebrews 10:35

I was calm and focused on my life plan with the system approach of continuous improvement. The more I did this, the more blessed I became. The resources I needed opened up to me at the right time. Commit to yourself and hold yourself accountable to your vision by changing your thought patterns and realising that practice makes progress.

The minute I changed my thought patterns to an awareness that my life is a sum of my thoughts, my emotions, and my choices, things started to shift for me.

For you, once you're clear about your North Star and committed to transforming your life into a purposeful and meaningful one, habits, even small ones, will lead you to change and close those gaps. This momentum will fuel your confidence and inspire you to keep going.

I believe you can do anything you put your mind to, because you have the power of infinite wisdom within.

I know I did, and I'm still working at it. I'm God's handiwork in progress, fearfully and wonderfully made. This is the gift of life. To experience it without regret—by being the author of your life story and owning your own thoughts—is the best thing you can do for yourself. The key ingredient that will keep you going is identity-based change, of who you are, and what your beliefs are. Who do you want to be in this life?

Are you committing to investing in your own self-development in order to support your authentic self?

You have the innate power to do anything you set your mind to. This comes from your internal source of infinite intelligence. You are special, and are loved unconditionally. You are enough to exist, contribute to the goodness of mankind, live in harmony, and have a purposeful life. This is our gift. It's an expression of love and belonging to a family beyond this earthly home.

ACKNOWLEDGEMENTS

I extend my deepest gratitude to the Passionpreneur team and to Moustafa. Thank you for your relentless pursuit of 'get the message to the world'. I'm extremely grateful to Clare for the words of encouragement and belief in my story, even at the tough point of starting this journey.

The completion and quality of this book wouldn't have been possible without Shobha's unwavering and nurturing guidance. My sincere thank you. I feel I have a friend and sister for life.

To my children, my number one fans. Your existence gives me strength. I appreciate your support, constant check-ups, and encouragement to stay the course. Your excitement fuelled my motivation.

To my person, my HB, thank you for giving me space and support to embark on this journey and being my sounding board and inspiration.

AUTHOR BIO

Victoria Moya is a trailblazer in the franchisee business world of South Africa, paving the way for aspiring female entrepreneurs. She has made significant contributions to the McDonald's franchise in South Africa. With a successfully growing business in the region, she received an Award as Operator of the Year in 2019.

Moya has applied her knowledge and business and psychology degrees towards 20+ years of experience in both corporate roles and self-owned business ventures. Her experiences span across financial services, FMCGs, and the QSR industry with a positive track record on customer excellence and operational efficiencies, including process methodology applications models yielding solid growth, and delivering value for shareholders.

Moya has also served as Chairman of South African National Leadership Council for the McDonald's Franchise and member of the McDonald's Global Chairman Leadership council. As Chairman, she has successfully represented South African franchisees on a global platform, which has enabled strategic alignment and critical policy changes, business model reviews, and culture alignments. She is also a motivational speaker, and her passion as a life coach is her way of giving back to the community.

Extras:

Website: www.iamvictoria.inc

Contact: info@iamvictoria.co

Notes

....

....

....

....

....

....

....

....

....

....

....

....

....

....

Milton Keynes UK
Ingram Content Group UK Ltd.
UKHW011435050524
442212UK00003B/31